Recovering Language in Higher Education

Laetitia Monbec · Alex Ding

Recovering Language in Higher Education

Social Justice, Ethics and Practices

Laetitia Monbec ⓘD
Language Centre, School
of Languages, Cultures and Societies
University of Leeds
Leeds, UK

Alex Ding ⓘD
Language Centre, School
of Languages, Cultures and Societies
University of Leeds
Leeds, UK

ISBN 978-3-031-76698-5   ISBN 978-3-031-76699-2   (eBook)
https://doi.org/10.1007/978-3-031-76699-2

Cover illustration: © John Rawsterne/patternhead.com

This Palgrave Macmillan imprint is published by the registered company Springer Nature Switzerland AG
The registered company address is: Gewerbestrasse 11, 6330 Cham, Switzerland

If disposing of this product, please recycle the paper.

Pour Lucette et Jacques

*Nous étouffons parmi les gens qui croient avoir absolument raison, que ce
soit dans leurs machines ou dans leurs idées. Et pour tous ceux qui ne
peuvent vivre que dans le dialogue et dans l'amitié des hommes, ce silence
est la fin du monde.*

Camus, A. (1946). Le siècle de la peur. Combat, *novembre*

*L'avi Siset em parlava
de bon matí al portal
mentre el sol esperàvem
i els carros vèiem passar.*

*Siset, que no veus l'estaca
on estem tots lligats?
Si no podem desfer-nos-en,
mai no podrem caminar!*

*Si estirem tots, ella caurà
i molt de temps no pot durar,
segur que tomba, tomba, tomba,
ben corcada deu ser ja.*

*Si tu l'estires fort per aquí,
i jo l'estiro fort per allà,
segur que tomba, tomba, tomba,
i ens podrem alliberar.*

(Extract from L'Estaca *, Lluís Llach 1968)*

ACKNOWLEDGMENT

In this book we have attempted to discuss our concerns and hopes for the fields of Language Teaching, English for Academic Purposes, and broadly for Higher Education through our complementary theoretical perspectives. While Alex has developed over several years a sociological and ethical analysis of the field and its practitioners, Laetitia has been concerned with knowledge blindness in language curriculum particularly around language ontology. Bringing together these interests, and casting complementary theoretical lenses, specifically Bourdieu's Field Theory, Ethics and Social Semiotics has made (we think) the outcome greater than the sum of its parts. We are grateful to Professor Sheena Gardner for generously sharing her expert advice and for taking the time to go through the manuscript. We are fortunate too for the support of colleagues at the Language Centre at the University of Leeds and beyond. We have been lucky over the years to meet colleagues across the world, who have engaged in friendly dialogue over the ideas in this volume. We value this dialogue above all.

As will be clear from each of the chapters, we are deeply indebted to the work of Pierre Bourdieu, Basil Bernstein, Michael Halliday, Ruqaiya Hasan, and Jim Martin (among many others). We hope readers will recognise themselves as fellow travellers (a term we take from Jim Martin).

PRAISE FOR *RECOVERING LANGUAGE IN HIGHER EDUCATION*

"Bernstein (1979: 300-1) challenged educators "to understand systematically how to create a concept which can authenticate the child's experience and give him or her those powerful representations of thought that he or she is going to need to change the world outside." This powerful, conscientious and self-conscious monograph by Monbec and Ding draws on Bourdieu, Social Semiotics and Ethics to engage directly with his challenge—filling the black hole of knowledge blindness in education with wisdom every teacher needs to know."

—Jim Martin, *Professor in Linguistics (Personal Chair), University of Sydney, Australia*

"Part I aims to break the illusio. It explains how we came to be where we are, by dissecting the role of language in the university system as we know it, in its neoliberalism, its attention to financialization, marketization and managerialism, and even in the fractioning of disciplines. As such, it is controversial. I imagine debating with students and colleagues claims such as "language is ... often misconstrued in the language classroom" or "adopting a 'radical' ... posture can be ... commodified both for the benefit of the academic and their university". As Monbec and Ding say, "the opinion and judgments expressed in the volume might go against readers' positions, or unquestioned thoughts." It is exquisitely detailed and referenced, but very recognisable and ultimately depressing. Chapter Four is a kind of pivot where different pedagogies are critiqued:

the liberal, conservative, radical and subversive. Then comes relief in the final chapters where language educators are presented as agents of change. We need to return to a focus on language as a semiotic resource and dispel the illusios. In this way we can develop EAP as a strong discipline respected across the university. On one level, this is a small step that can only begin the wider change needed, but it is a step that we can take in a socially just and ethical manner that enables us to begin that journey, to share a view of language and how it construes disciplinary worlds and lead to change in the role of language across the university. Thank you, Laetitia and Alex, for a welcome call to action!"

—Sheena Gardner, *Professor of Applied Linguistics, University of Coventry, UK*

"In this excellent work, Laetitia Monbec and Alexander Ding take the ontological realism of Bernstein, Bourdieu and Bhaskar and apply it rapier-like to the cankerous and fetid knowledge regime that is neoliberal higher education. Not only do they break the illusio, but they also offer new lines of thinking and action for language specialists working in this domain. A profound critical intervention."

—John P. O'Regan, *Professor of Critical Applied Linguistics, University College London, UK*

"This is work that is simultaneously courageous and cautious, as it seeks to meet the broader threats that higher education faces with a model of language teaching that empowers both teachers and students. Bringing together Bourdieu's Field Theory and Social Semiotics to map out the possibilities for agency that academics still have in such choppy waters, the authors balance their critique of existing approaches with an awareness of their own audacity. The suggestion that we can still reclaim some space in our classrooms and in the interstices of our institutions to speak back against the erasure of knowledge is an inspiring one. With its blend of theoretical insight and practical resources, the book offers a way forward."

—Dr Shobha Avadhani, *Senior Lecturer, Department of Communication and New Media, National University of Singapore*

"The pervasive logics of neoliberalism in higher education has functioned to strip academics of tools and dispositions to act as agents of change in a social world in dire need for hope, solidarity, and deeper meaning. Linguistics and language education remain no exception to this trend, partly due to the continued influence of linguistic and pedagogical ontologies that uphold ideologically neutral views of the relationship between language, education, and society. This volume develops and illustrates a principled approach to tackling social justice endeavors through language education. It proposes a powerful articulation and critique of sociological, social semiotic, and ethical principles that extends the fields' collective knowledge base for mobilizing multiliterate multisemiotic praxis within and beyond universities. The authors' balanced deconstruction of dominant beliefs and practices sets the scene for critical discussions that recenter language as a privileged site for building a more just, solidary and hopeful social order. More broadly, it contributes a timely manifesto for socially committed educational linguistics amidst our pressing global conjunctures."

—Dr. Jesús Guerra-Lyons, *Language Institute-Universidad del Norte, Colombia*

CONTENTS

About the Authors

Dr. Laetitia Monbec is Lecturer and the Director of Scholarship at the Language Centre at the University of Leeds. She has worked at the National University of Singapore, and at City University of Hong Kong designing and teaching various English for Academic Purposes and CLIL programmes. Her research has investigated the impact of systemic functional linguistics/genre pedagogy in EAP, disciplinary discourse specifically in Biological Sciences, in Design, and in Nursing, Critical Thinking, Multimodality and colour semiotics.

Dr. Alex Ding is Professor of English for Academic Purposes. Co-author of 'The English for Academic Purposes Practitioner: Operating on the Edge of Academia'. He has recently co-edited, 'Social Theory for English for Academic Purposes' and 'Practitioner Agency and Identity in English for Academic Purposes'. He also co-leads the MA in Teaching English for Academic Purposes at the University of Leeds.

LIST OF FIGURES

LIST OF TABLES

CHAPTER 1

Introduction: Social Theory, Linguistics and Ethics for Change

Abstract This introductory chapter positions the volume within discussions around the role of language and language educators in social justice and social transformation endeavours. The chapter explains the usefulness of a clear language ontology such as social semiotics, a social theory such as Bourdieu's Field Theory and Ethics in these discussions. The chapter argues this knowledge base is necessary for educators to critically reflect on their practice and to impact their students and the broader academic field. It concludes with a preview of the chapters in the volume.

Keywords Social change · Language education · Social semiotics · Systemic Functional Linguistics · Ethics · Bourdieu's field theory · Illusio

The volume provides a theoretical and practical discussion of the role language, social theory and ethics can play in understanding and enhancing socially committed teaching and scholarship. The abundance of publications on social justice in language education attests to language teachers' core concern to use their position within higher education to bring about change. Yet, despite decades of publications about critical pedagogy, or about neoliberalism in universities, no clear solutions present themselves. This volume positions social theory, semiotics and ethics as the necessary knowledge base educators need to enable daily

L. Monbec and A. Ding, *Recovering Language in Higher Education*, https://doi.org/10.1007/978-3-031-76699-2_1

decisions that can have a positive impact. In doing so, the volume also extends current debates around social justice and social change in and through education, arguing that language (and more broadly multimodal meaning-making), social theory and ethics, are key to understanding and addressing these debates productively. The volume weaves accessible theoretical discussions with practical applications and provides the reader with an opportunity to critically examine their own beliefs in relation to language, values and pedagogies underpinning their practice, and the heterodoxic practices in the field. It then develops a model for language educators which includes a widened and more specialised knowledge around a clarified ontology of language and meaning-making, a collective sociological understanding of the field, and a concerted and shared reflexive orientation to the ethics and practices of language and literacy provision in higher education. In this sense, the volume is both ambitious and prosaic, both theoretical and practical.

The title 'to *recover* language' refers to a central argument in the volume, that language is woefully misunderstood as a resource for change, and often misconstrued in language classrooms and the wider university but that it is in fact a foundational element in any attempts at improving practices and reviving academic ethos.

Educators Between Cynicism, Hope and Despair

Reflecting the frustration and the complexity of the task, the volume might appear like an emotional roller-coaster. The ills of higher education are well documented (Collini, 2017; Ding & Bruce, 2017): the demands of academic work, the precarity and mismanagement have left the sector grasping for meaning. Students are tired, overworked, assessed, graded, marked and surveyed to death. Educational systems conflate competition with distinction, and by trying to reduce the first, throw away excellence and high standards. Evidence of impact is evaluated with flawed criteria, and whole departments are periodically vandalised by senior management who have neither the understanding, nor the ethics or wisdom to be given such responsibility (Collini, 2017). University discourse is imbued with social justice values, decolonising, care, diversity, equity, representation but delivers unfit solutions in outsourced (at eye-watering cost) consultant workshops. These key terms are used to design brochures by neoliberal managements concerned with a branding that keeps attracting fee-paying students. The imperative to adapt to change (Stiegler, 2023) has academics go through continual turns, and fads, while critical engagement is framed as lack of cooperation and anti-progressiveness. Adding to the alienation, and the increasingly busy weeks, educators must sit in tedious well-being training workshops to develop individual resilience and self-care strategies proposed through colourful mindmaps listing meditation or pets. In a flat ontological world, only the empirical exists, there are no hidden causes.

The impact these systemic factors have on individual and collective agents has been damaging, both exacerbating the least dignified of human penchant and closing the actual potential for individual and collective action. It's not just managements who distort concepts and empty them of any transformational potential. Scholars also often acquiesce to the same logic and play a self-serving (or self-preserving) game. They might, for example, appropriate the current discourse, by turning their distress into navel-gazing research. Autoethnography and the lived experience, have been presented as a humanist approach to research (which they can be) but, when distorted, mask a compulsive need to talk about oneself, and—less charitably—a strategy for the privileged to benefit from the current management-endorsed discourse. Research metrics have also led to an exponential growth of publications which add little to meaningful knowledge. Social media abounds with academic accounts that broadcast success, rewards and promotions, or share monoglossic injunctions, tautological aphorisms and platitudes asserted to position oneself rather than engage in dialogue.

Awareness and understanding of these issues need not lead to despair, however, and this book is far from cynical. Universities are still a privileged space for critical thinking, where collegiality, collectivity and solidarity can help hope stay alive (Collini, 2017). Universities still offer the joy to interact with students, a meaningful mission to build and share knowledge, to read and engage in dialogue. Indeed, if we look carefully, we are also, still, presented every day with choices that can have impact. The aim of the volume then is to argue that despite the constraints highlighted, language educators can be agents of change. The ideas in this volume derive from our educational practices and contexts, from conversations, exchange of readings and critiques and the complementary orientation of the two authors, one towards social theory and philosophy, the other towards systemic functional linguistics and social semiotics. The key scholars whose work developed our thinking are Pierre Bourdieu, Ruqaiya Hasan, Basil Bernstein, Michael Halliday, Jim Martin, Theo van

Leeuwen and many others including beyond sociology and linguistics. Their ideals and ethos we hope echo through the volume.

Social Theory, Social Semiotics and Ethics

The ambitious goal of positioning language educators as agents of change calls for robust theoretical tools to analyse the broadest to the smallest of phenomena. First, as Bhaskar argues, 'change cannot occur unless we understand the structures that operate the events that lead to how things are' (Bhaskar, 1989, p. 2). Bourdieu agrees 'we must provide causal explanations to "make trouble" and "provoke"; that is, to question received categories and unveil the doxic taken-for-granted assumptions of the social world that typically conceal power relations' (Bourdieu, 1993). Go (2023) argues it is important to consider the historical element of the causal relation. This is what we tried to do in Ding and Monbec (2024) when we began the socio-analysis of the English for Academic Purposes field through a discourse analysis of its narratives of origins which we argued sets up these types of causal relations which are justifications for value systems and practices still influential today.

In the exploration of these causal relations, a key concept we start with is Bourdieu's *illusio*. In Bourdieu's words, we need to know 'How things [come to be] the way they are?'. This, in Bourdieu's theory consists in 'breaking the illusio', a challenging task because the illusio is constituted of fundamental and implicit beliefs and routine actions. Illusio refers to 'the enchanted circle of collective denial' (Bourdieu, 2000: 5). It justifies and consists of our investments in our field (whatever it may be, EAP, Academic Literacy, Higher Education), our ways of being taken in by the stakes, the logic of the field (Bourdieu, 2000).

> The game presents itself to someone caught up in it, absorbed in it, as a transcendent universe, imposing its own ends and norms unconditionally [...], and the illusio is an illusion or 'diversion' only for someone who perceives the game from the outside, from a scholastic standpoint of an 'impartial spectator'.
>
> (Bourdieu, 2000, p. 151)

Bourdieu's Field Theory provides the theoretical and analytical tools to investigate the field of higher education and language education specifically: its values, and ethos, its legitimation practices and means of reproduction. Bourdieu's theory, as encompassing as it is, does not extend into a workable linguistics which would explain linguistically how social structure is reproduced. For this, we must lean on a social theory of language, a linguistics that can do the job ontologically, theoretically and analytically. The second element of our theoretical toolkit then is a linguistics that can account for social phenomena as being construed and enacted through semiosis. The only theory we found up to the task is Social Semiotics, a social theory of meaning-making which draws extensively on the work of Michael Halliday, Ruqaiya Hasan and Jim Martin and many others within Systemic Functional Linguistics/Semiotics.

Briefly here, we will explain why SFL is a linguistics that is well-equipped for analysing the role of language in social reproduction and to think of its potential for social change. The discussion below might appear abstract, but Chapter 2 explains these ideas in detail. For Hasan, and several other functional linguists who appear in the volume, 'language is a shaper of reality [which] is to say that language is instrumental in sustaining this suspension of disbelief' (Hasan, 1996, p. 16), a notion closely related to Bourdieu's *illusio*. Language is key both in creating and in maintaining social structures and worldviews. This language ontology provides the theoretical tools to consider language as social action, and it provides the descriptive apparatus to delve into the internal workings of language from the smallest unit of analysis at phonological or lexicogrammatical level, to the broadest elements of discourse semantics and genre. It is through this connected architecture that we can then explain social reproduction and world construal, that we can make sense of urgent phenomena such as the destruction of our planet's environment, and the recurrent rise of tyranny, and anti-democratic, authoritarian ideologies that rely so much on a strategic use of language. For this reason alone, a linguistic theory that sees semiotics as the engine of ideology, is crucial. Beyond these more visible and well-documented effects of language within political discourse, even more crucial to educators, is a linguistics theory that explains how semiotics develops our consciousness, and so builds our mental categories, from, *inter alia,* scientific knowledge classifications, divisions of (living) things into gender, people into race, sectioning of the visible light spectrum into hues, construal of natural resources as plentiful or positioning of humans as dominating the natural world (see Chapter 2 for more on this). Unfortunately, common conceptions of language are often limited to discussions of standards, accuracy, and appropriacy of writing (rather than meaning-making) as social practice, even within language education circles. This volume argues that understanding the power of language and semiotics to shape and construe our world, is everyone's responsibility, at home, in schools and universities, and in every discipline.

Bourdieu's Field Theory combined with Systemic Functional Semiotics then allows us to keep the social and the semiotics in sight with theories that broadly align on the relation between language and society (see Ding & Monbec, 2024). One direction in this relation, from the social to the semiotics, is perhaps better researched and understood. In this volume we are also interested in the other direction, from the semiotics to the social, in other words on ways language use can impact and change the broader social realm. If as Bourdieu writes: 'the whole social structure is present in each interaction' (Bourdieu, 1991, p. 67), and language is a key element in social reproduction, can deliberate use of language or semiotics disrupt social reproduction, effect social change? Hasan argues that 'This suspension of disbelief towards the linguistically shaped reality is capable of being disturbed only to the extent that within language also lies the possibility of raising questions, of constructing arguments, of demanding proofs' (Hasan, 1996, p. 23). Halliday saw the possibility of every act of meaning to 'destroy[s]and recreate[s]' the system—'almost identically, but not quite' (Halliday, 2002, p. 152). For Halliday, then, every semiotic act can impact the world, and he argued that language has evolved to construe our world the way it now appears, with its issues and challenges, and that this evolution is ongoing. Our linguistic choices then, are still shaping people's consciousness and potentially participate to social change (Halliday, 2003:217). Others have developed these ideas: Martin, and Bartlett for example, explore through positive discourse analysis ways discourse is used to achieve change (Bartlett, 2017; Martin, 2004) or conceive of disruption in semiotics as impacting the context of communication by legitimising alternative meaning-making practices and coding orientations (see Bartlett's 2013 concept of *perturbation potential*).

Hasan (1995, p. 249), however, is doubtful:

> . . . to imagine that, by revealing disjunctions, we could bring about revolutions, does appear to me somewhat grandiose. It suggests quite wrongly that the material effects of past semiosis – the institutions, practices and systems of belief that have been created through interactions using various semiotic modalities – are so insubstantial as 'to keel over' at our new and daring verbal semiotic adventures in combining the uncombinable!

It might, as Hasan writes, appear naïve, but it also seems that when it comes to spreading hateful ideologies and appealing to, revealing or energising the basest of human instinct, deliberate rhetoric strategies are fantastically effective at shaping consciousness and the material world. Work in critical discourse analysis has had great success in making visible the ways language legitimises state violence, dehumanises certain communities, silences victims and protects abusers—knowledge which has now become mainstream. We only need to observe the backlash to these dents in the doxic semiotic fabric to understand how close these hit those who benefit from the way things are. If language is actively used to maintain the status quo; can it not be actively taught to change it? This is a key question we address in the volume, with complementary social theory and semiotics lenses which conceive agency in similar ways, within constraints (of habitus or semantic orientation) but with possibility to disrupt the social and linguistic systems with every act and meaning-making instance.

As the reader will note from the title of the volume and the chapters, ethics is also part of our theoretical framework, as an essential element in effecting change. Ethics completes the sociological and semiotic view by bringing in individual responsibility. It enables an analysis of the lack of response to, even the compliance from academics with current higher education. More importantly it is key to individual and collective agency and to restoring hope that individual action can impact the collective, and the structure.

The volume is organised into two parts. Part 1 *Breaking the illusio* considers language ontology, ethos and pedagogy as main elements of the illusio and attempts to tease out false dichotomies.

Chapter 2, *Language ontology as illusio,* aims to enable readers to surface and question conceptions of the nature of language (or ontological beliefs) within their specific field, and in relation to their own educational practices. After outlining the main characteristics of two broad ontologies (language as rule vs language as resource) and explaining why one is dominant, or default, the chapter explores the ways these beliefs, often tacit, shape common discourse around language, educational policies and educational practices such as needs analysis, curriculum design, the teaching of grammar and assessment. The chapter also argues that ontology vagueness or implicitness helps perpetuate language ideologies such as 'ideal competence', 'deficit' views of language learners and native speakerism in language teaching. The chapter aims to bring ontological clarity to the forefront of language policy planning and language teaching practices.

Chapter 3, *Illusio and Ethos in Academia,* provides an analysis of the ethos of academics in neoliberal universities with the aim to develop an *ethics* for academics. More than adding to the large literature dissecting the nefarious impact of neoliberalism, the chapter critiques academics' lack of collective response to the higher education crisis. Framing the discussion around three key factors, which, since the 1980s, have changed the ethos, structures, and roles of universities—namely financialisation, marketisation and managerialism, the chapter uses Bourdieu's concept of *illusio* to help explain the apparent complicity of academics to reproduce neoliberal practices. Reasons advanced include that of epistemopathy: that knowledge, especially of impending doom, leads to disempowerment. Another key explanation is that neoliberal 'rules of the game' (such as pressure, control, rewards and punishment) only accentuated what was already there: academics' inherent desire for symbolic capital. In fact, the chapter exemplifies complicit behaviours from resignation, radical or critical posturing, increased incivility, to prodigious publication metrics, which show both a loss of meaning and a threat to (or loss of) illusio. The chapter concludes that it is through the difficult and long process of transforming academic habitus that we have any chance of transforming universities.

Chapter 4, *Changing the world from the classroom: Pedagogy as illusio,* explores pedagogical approaches in language teaching that have social justice aspirations. Using Basil Bernstein's (1996) pedagogies typology (liberal, conservative, radical, subversive) to enable systematic comparison around visibility and knowledge, the chapter teases out false dichotomies that pit conservative against radical approaches, foreclosing other options. The chapter clarifies terms such as *critical* pedagogy, a term often assigned to very different practices that only converge around a professed but vague social justice goal. The chapter provides an in-depth critique of Critical English for Academic Purposes, and Raciolinguistics as influential manifestations of *radical* pedagogies within the field of literacy. It also critiques Systemic Functional Linguistics/Genre, Reflective Literacy and variations of Critical Literacy as examples of *subversive* pedagogies. The chapter concludes with a means of reconciliation around concepts such as repertoire and registers, around language as a mode of critical social action, and with a call for a literacy approach that equips students with the necessary knowledge to *both* access powerful discourse and 'play the game', *and* to raise consciousness of the role of language not only in social reproduction but also in broader democratic destabilisation drives and global crises.

Chapter 5, *Heresy, Ethics and Scholarship,* focuses on '*doing something*' *within* language education in universities. The chapter draws, specifically, on our own field English for Academic Purposes (EAP) and develops an *ethics* for language educators. Starting from the need to conduct socio-analyses as groundwork for change, the chapter details a socio-analysis of the field of EAP which illuminates forms of injustices and domination. It argues this can trigger an informed and collective response by revealing potential choices and possibilities for the future—a form of heresy. The chapter sees scholarship as central to this ethics, and redefines it as broader than SoTL, and free from neoliberal imperatives that plague research. This ethics also requires engaging critically with agents in the field. Finally, this ethics argues for a developed knowledge base that allows practitioners a potent specialism and role within universities. In EAP, this means making visible the entanglements of academic communication within disciplinary epistemological and social forces to disciplinary colleagues and students, with potential (ethical) changes in disciplinary communication practices in teaching, in research, and in policies and practices.

Chapter 6 outlines an expanded knowledge base for educators which we see as key to support agency and social change. Chapter 6, *Educating for Agency and Solidarity: A social semiotics knowledge base,* describes powerful knowledge to develop positive, critical multiliteracies, valuing differences to build solidarity. The chapter explains what a functional language ontology looks like in curriculum and teaching practice. Leaning on Systemic Functional Linguistics, Systemic Functional Semiotics and Legitimation Code Theory, the chapter details a body of semiotics resources from Genre, Discourse Semantics and Lexicogrammar to multi-modality, register variety and knowledge which a language educator can use both to analyse their students and disciplinary colleagues needs (in EAP contexts for example) and to design curriculum which develops agency and criticality. Examples are provided from disciplines such as Engineering and the School of Music, along with a step-by-step guide to analyse a complex genre, the lecture recital, engaging this multi-framework toolkit. The chapter concludes that beyond the ethics and scholarship advocated in the previous chapter, this type of expanded knowledge base can help develop practitioners' impact on student learning, but also their capital, status and influence.

This book might appear controversial to some. We do not believe it is, although the opinion and judgments expressed in the volume might go against readers' positions or unquestioned thoughts. While it might seem scathing in parts, the two authors are not exempt from any of the harsh judgments made. We are epistemic agents just like the academics we critique in these pages, as likely to act as our position in the field allows and dictates as others, unless a real effort at reflexivity is exercised (and in this we do not claim best practice). The book might also appear polemical because it uses a rhetorical strategy that Bourdieu has called 'twisting the screw the other way' (Bourdieu, 1990, p. 53) which by showing reality in an exaggerated form can be seen as a sacrilege (see Ding & Monbec, 2024). If the volume generates any of these reactions (hopefully along with some positive ones), we hope readers will engage with the ideas, and that discussions and proper debates will flourish (Hammersley, 2023). For our part, we trust we have written with honesty about what we see as within our power to act upon—our agency to effect change as language teachers: agency over *what* we teach and over *ways* we teach it, and agency over our professional and personal ethos.

REFERENCES

Bartlett, T. (2013). "I'll manage the context": Context, environment and the potential for institutional change. In L. Fontaine, T. Bartlett, & G. O'Grady (Eds.), *Systemic functional linguistics: Exploring choice* (pp. 342–364). Cambridge University Press.

Bartlett, T. (2017). Context in systemic functional linguistics: Towards scalar supervenience? In T. Bartlett, & G. O'Grady (Eds), *The Routledge handbook of systemic functional linguistics* (pp. 399–414). Routledge.

Bernstein, B. (1996). *Pedagogy, symbolic control, and identity: Theory, research, critique*. Taylor & Francis.

Bhaskar, R. (1989). *Reclaiming reality: A critical introduction to contemporary philosophy*. Verso Book.

Bourdieu, P. (1990). *The logic of practice*. Cambridge: Polity Press.

Bourdieu, P. (1991). *Language and symbolic power*. Harvard University Press.

Bourdieu, P. (1993). *Sociology in question*. Sage.

Bourdieu, P. (2000). *Pascalian meditations*. Stanford University Press.

Collini, S. (2017). *Speaking of universities*. Verso Books.

Ding, A., & Bruce, I. (2017). *The English for academic purposes practitioner: Operating on the edge of academia*. Palgrave Macmillan.

Ding, A., & Monbec, L. (2024). A socio-analysis of English for academic purposes. In A. Ding & L. Monbec (Eds.), *Practitioner agency and identity in English for academic purposes.* Bloomsbury.

Go, J. (2023). Unveiling power, or why social science's task is explanation. *The British Journal of Sociology.* https://doi.org/10.1111/1468-4446.13056

Hasan, R. (1995). The conception of context in text. In P. Fries & M. Gregory (Eds.), *Discourse in society: Systemic functional perspectives: Meaning and choice in language: Studies for Michael Halliday* (pp. 183–283). Ablex.

Hasan, R. (1996). *Ways of saying: Ways of meaning: Selected papers of Ruqaiya Hasan (C. Cloran, D. Butt, & G. Williams, Eds.).* Bloomsbury Academic.

Halliday, M. A. K. (2002). Poetry as scientific discourse: The nuclear sections of Tennyson's In Memoriam. In J. J. Webster (Ed.), *Linguistic studies of text and discourse: Volume 2 in the collected works of M.A.K. Halliday* (pp. 149–167). Continuum.

Halliday, M. A. K. (2003). *On language and linguistics.* (Vol.3). In J. J. Webster (Ed.), The collected works of M.A.K. Halliday (pp. 1–15). Continuum.

Hammersley, M. (2023). *Methodological concepts: A critical guide.* Routledge.

Martin, J. R. (2004). Positive discourse analysis: Power, solidarity and change. *Revista Canaria De Estudios Ingleses, 49,* 179–200.

Stiegler, B. (2023). *«Il faut s'adapter»: Sur un nouvel impératif politique.* Gallimard.

PART I

Breaking the Illusio

CHAPTER 2

Language Ontology as Illusio

Abstract This chapter aims to enable readers to surface and question conceptions of the nature of language (or ontological beliefs) within their specific field, and in relation to their own educational practices. After outlining the main characteristics of two broad ontologies (language as rule vs language as resource) and explaining why one is dominant, or default, the chapter explores the ways these beliefs, often tacit, shape common discourse around language, educational policies, educational or classroom practices such as needs analysis, curriculum design, the teaching of grammar and assessment. The chapter also argues that ontology vagueness or implicitness helps perpetuate language ideologies such as 'ideal competence', 'deficit' views of language learners and native speakerism in language teaching. The chapter aims to bring ontology to the forefront of scholarship, language policy planning and language teaching practices.

Keywords Language ontology · Linguistic theories · Systemic Functional Semiotics · Formal Linguistics · Competence · Deficit view · Language learning · Ideology · Native speakerism · Consciousness · Language teaching practices

Underlying every language education program is some view of language. That very often this view of language is a taken for granted view, seemingly

never in need of being explicitly debated or discussed, suggests that it is a
dominant view of language, which voices official ideology.
Hasan, 2011, p. 29.

Introduction: Language Ontology as a Blindspot

This chapter explores the ways underlying conceptions of the nature of
language—ontological beliefs—shape educational practices in language
teaching in higher education. It discusses the different conceptions of
language reflected in pedagogical practices, in policies and in general
discourse about language. It examines the factors that might shape
these ontological, and ideological, beliefs about language. It considers
what ontological knowledge about language education practitioners and
scholars might lean on to make their practice as reflective and impactful
as they wish it to be. These issues seem important to explore because
ontological beliefs about language have direct impact on *what can* be
known about language, and therefore what is seen as language teachers
and educational practitioners' remit. They have a direct impact on *what
can* and will be taught, and on the types of solutions to educational
issues that can be devised. They then have a direct consequence on
the social impact of language teaching at large. Yet, countless publications in language teaching, applied linguistic and sociolinguistics exhibit
ontological vagueness, or worse, ontological confusion.

A lack of ontological clarity impacts far beyond educational practices.
Ontological clarity is related to an awareness of how language functions,
what it does in/to our world and how it shapes our consciousness. It
shapes how language is positioned as more or less legitimate not only in
curriculums but ultimately within human knowledge. Specific ontological
alignment, for example, might enable us to consider language at the heart
of the undoing of our societies and our natural world and so becomes
crucial to anyone concerned with educating for agency, social justice and
transformation. To take an urgent example of the ways language impacts
our world, we can use authoritarians' use of language, which is well
documented (Klemperer, 2006; Snyder, 2017; Alvaro, 2014). Far-right
populists use language deliberately to dehumanise certain communities,
to muddle issues, to conflate and slide discourses—for example the drift
from narratives of environmental protection to ecofascist ideas and climate
change denial (Szenes, 2021). Language is key to legitimising the most

inhumane state sponsored violence and war (Lukin, 2019). Naomi Klein's *Doppelganger* (2023) provides a chilling account of far-right strategists destabilising democratic societies with conspiracy theories that hook onto (more or less) legitimate fears and frustration to mirror and distort them. Their key weapon is manipulation of language, especially the capacity to 'capture' words ('pipik' in Klein's book) which were once clear but which under deliberate meaning distortion are stripped of their power (recalling Orwell's *1984* Newspeak which not only breaks the link between sign and signified, but also progressively erases words in order to constrain thinking). Klein demonstrates that '[a]bsolutely anything and anyone can be severed from their contexts and made to mean their precise opposite' (Klein, 2023, p. 156). At the time of writing, we had just come across the term *ecofascism* being claimed (pipiked) by climate change sceptics to label policies aimed at protecting the environment. This is a world then, where words we used to trust with a well understood meaning such as *'fascism'*, can be made to mean very little anymore, having been captured by actual fascists to describe anti-fascist movements. Other similar words are *genocide*, or *terrorist*. This is also a world where the sentence *'you can't say anything these days'* decries intransigent self-righteousness (that solidarity-breaking exploitation of identity politics, and distracting outrage at minor infractions), but is also invoked to brush over abject sexist and racist practices—language conflates behaviours that are absolutely not the same. Language strategies then are an effective staple in nefarious political movements...whether the same power can be harnessed to develop protection against these strategies, to build agency and empower is a question that threads throughout this book. Maybe it is doubtful that the impact language has on perceptions translates readily into material changes (Klein, 2023), but it remains that language and semiotics are often where visible battles occur. Perhaps what can be affirmed here is first that the less we know about language, the less we can defend its value, and that language is people's **only** accessible powerful tool. This brings educational practitioners, language teachers and scholars in higher education to the forefront if language education is to embrace a more proactive, constructive and positive mission. To do this, there is a need to explore in more depth what we understand language to be—in other words, language ontology.

This chapter then aims to enable readers to question language ontological beliefs within their specific field, and in relation to their own educational practices. To do this, we first define language ontology, and explain why a degree of clarity matters to anyone concerned with educa-tion. We advance a few reasons why language ontology is rarely a focus of language teacher's knowledge base. We then outline the main charac-teristics of two broad language ontological strands and their implication in practice: a psychological/philosophical strand (exemplified partly here by Formal Grammar, and Transformative-Generative Grammar) on the one hand, and a social/ethnographic strand (represented mostly in this chapter by Systemic Functional Linguistics/Semiotics) on the other hand, as they represent a rift still current in conceptions, teaching practices and academic discussions around language and linguistics (Seargeant, 2010). In part 2, we outline some repercussions of these ontological assumptions on (1) ideologies such as the notion of 'ideal competence', the deficit view of language and learners, the 'zombie-like' native speakerism ideology, language learning approaches and the mischaracterisation of academic writing as well as in (2) practices such as needs analysis, curriculum design, the teaching of grammar and assessment.

Language ontology refers to *the nature of language*, its properties, composition, structures and relations, the type of phenomenon it is. Ontology does not only question external relations and how language relates to speakers and society, but its internal properties too. Ruqaiya Hasan's quote at the start of the chapter underlines how understanding our practices and their impact, requires us to unpack our unthought thoughts about language. Curriculum, assessment and pedagogical prac-tices and policy cannot be divorced from what we believe language to be. Hall and Wicaksono (2020) explain the importance of developing a clear ontological understanding of language:

> Leaving our conceptualisations unexamined and unacknowledged creates the potential for flawed reasoning, missed opportunities to recognise (in)compatibilities between different positions, and the perpetuation of ill-considered recommendations for policy and practice (2020, p. 4).

Leaving our conceptualisations unexamined makes language educators vulnerable to misrecognition of educational problems and misleads us in our search for solutions. Ontological questions are not anodyne, and linguistic theories are not neutral knowledge. They normalise language practices and beliefs. Ignoring or treating our ontological views as having no impact on shaping our practices can disempower us. Moreover, we might 'in abstraction' align broadly with a functional ontology (for example), but not actually enact it in many of our practices. There might well be excellent reasons for a varied pedagogical approach which reflects different language ontologies, but dogmatic and hegemonic practices can conceal themselves comfortably within eclectic approaches, making impactful change difficult to achieve.

At fault for this knowledge blind spot is a combination of factors, including language teacher training, and varying entry qualifications, as Ding and Bruce (2017) discuss in relation to English for Academic Purposes (EAP). Programmes for the DELTA[1] qualification, for example, tend to emphasise theories of language acquisition (rather than language), teaching approaches (including esoteric ones like the Silent Way, an approach the DELTA syllabus calls 'experimental and non-mainstream') and teaching skills, such as planning and delivering lessons, but include limited knowledge about language (DELTA Syllabus, 2022). The time devoted to language on Masters in EAP and TESOL programmes or ELT qualifications we surveyed seems to only allow for hasty attention to ontology (one module on 'Language' if anything, and often skewed towards one linguistic theory or SLA). This is confirmed in the US, where language teacher preparation courses tend to introduce students to structural linguistics, and psycholinguistics only (Accurso, 2019). In any case, much of teacher development occurs ad-hoc in their professional setting. As Acevedo observes, 'teachers' theoretical orientations to learning are often tacitly acquired through observation and participation in longstanding classroom routines, allowing them to become 'naturalised' as commonly held 'folk theories' (Kövecses, 2002, p. 109) which often remain unexamined' (Acevedo, 2020, p. 29). When much of the ELT, TESOL and EAP core literature pays little attention to clarifying various language ontologies, ad-hoc professional development is unlikely to help in this area. If, as Coffin and Donohue (2014) argue, language in higher education is invisible, the 'medium in which we swim', then we language educators swim in doxic water which obscures the nature and the potential of what we teach and through which we teach.

Language ontology is the first *illusio* the volume addresses.

---

[1] There is no space to discuss the DELTA syllabus, but a cursory look at the official syllabus confirms there is, for a language teaching qualification, a limited attention to knowledge about language. The focus is strongly on teaching skills, classroom management, language learning theories and management of EFL language programmes.

Defining and Contrasting Language Ontologies

In philosophy, the nature of language has been investigated in relation to the nature of meaning and intentionality, interaction with the world and reference, relation between language, consciousness, thought, truth and reality, and also its architecture, including parts of speech and syntax (Blackburn, 1995). Speculation about the nature of language has a long history which Robbins (2013) begins with the Indian scholar, Pāṇini's Sanskrit grammar, followed by scholars in ancient Greece. Volumes on the history of Linguistics such as Sampson's (1980) describe a field characterised by a multitude of schools. In the end of the nineteenth and the twentieth centuries alone, in the Western traditions, 'schools' include Structuralists (de Saussure), Functional Linguistics and the Prague School (Jakobson, Mathesius), the American anthropological approaches (Boas, Sapir, Whorf, Haas, Pike) structuralists/descriptivists (Harris, Bloomsfield), Generative Grammar (Chomsky), Relational Grammar and Stratificational Linguistics (Hjelmslev, Lamb), the London School (Firth), Scale and Category grammar (Gregory), Functional Systemic and neo-Firthian approaches (Halliday, Hasan, Matthiessen, Martin), Cognitive linguistics (Lakoff), Ecolinguistics (Stibbe) and Social Actor Theory (Van Leeuwen).

What matters most for our purpose is that linguistic theories enact language ontologies through their theoretical and analytical categories (Seargeant, 2009). Lukin explains how 'across the spectrum of linguistic theories, we find varying conceptions about the nature of language: what it is, how it works, and how it relates to human experience of the world' (Lukin, 2019, p.33). What further complicates matters in a discipline like Linguistics is the challenge of 'comparing like with like' when different categorisations and kinds of data underpin grammatical description (Martin, Doran and Figueredo, 2020).

The following are several ontological constructs which we see as key to educational contexts, and which can provide a means to compare theories:

(1) The *nature of the phenomenon* itself and how to best understand it: a natural phenomenon to be studied as a natural science, or a social phenomenon to be studied as a social semiotics?

(2) Of particular importance for educators concerned with social transformation and agency is *the nature of the relation (if any) between language and thought, consciousness, cognition, and with 'reality', the social world and ideology.* Some theories see no relation at all, while

others align to different degrees with a conception of language as shaping, reflecting, construing, constructing, reproducing the social world and ideology and organising our perception of the world.

(3) The *comprehensiveness/scope* of the theory architecture and its relation to other theories. For example, does it theorise beyond sentence level grammar and encompass discourse, lexicogrammar, phonology, or is it mostly concerned with syntax? Does it attempt to theorise meaning and relation to elements beyond language, such as social context, or users, or does it defer to other disciplines such as pragmatics, semantics, sociolinguistics and various philosophy, psychology, cognitive sciences, pragmatics-aligned frameworks such as Gricean maxims, speech act theory, relevance theory, conversation analysis? And if yes, are these additional frameworks explicit about the language ontology they adopt (see Hasan's, 2011 analysis of Pragmatics).

(4) The *applicability of the theory*: is it meant to address world problems (educational or other) and what does it see the remit of Linguistics to be?

(5) The way *language is learnt* and the role language plays in learning processes.

Two broad strands emerge from synthesising accounts: the philosophical/psychological and the descriptive/ethnographic strands following the terminology used in Martin (1982) and Halliday (2003). From the perspective of teaching/learning, Halliday explains: 'the former represents *language as rules*; it stresses the formal analysis of sentence and uses for purposes of idealisation (for deciding what falls within or outside its scope) the criterion of grammaticality (what is, or is not, according to the rule). The latter represents *language as a resource* and as choice; it stresses the semantic interpretation of discourse and uses for idealisation purposes the criterion of acceptability or usage (what occurs or could be envisaged to occur)' (Halliday, 2003). Table 2.1 provides an illustration of these two strands along the ontological constructs explained above to guide readers' interrogation of their own beliefs and practices.

Table 2.1 A comparison of 'language as rule' and 'language as resource' ontologies

Philosophical/psychological, formal strand Language as rule	Criteria	Ethnographic/sociological, functional strand Language as resource
A cognitive phenomenon	**Nature of the phenomenon**	A social semiotic resource for meaning-making
Universality: what makes languages alike (or like English)	**Focus**	Variability: what makes language(s) different
Language as rule Ideal standard leads to focus on form Focus on form	**Influence on language pedagogical practices**	Language as resource Focus on function Language in use, as a system of choices focus on meaning and *how* we mean within social context
Theoretical Linguistics Branch of cognitive psychology	**Type of theory**	Appliable Linguistics Social theory of language in use; language-based linguistics
Ideal Competence Universal Grammar Performance	**Key theoretical concepts**	For SFL: Choice, systems, strata, paradigmatic view, instantiation, metafunctions
Architecture theorises levels of grammar/syntax and phonology. Separate frameworks theorise pragmatics, semantics, cognition Invented sentences Meaning is not the object of study Prioritises syntagmatic approach (rules to sequence structure)	**Architecture scope and object of study**	Architecture includes context, discourse, lexicogrammar, phonology Naturally occurring language Meaning is the core concern (units and object of study can be above the clause, and can include visual, aural, kinetic semiotic resources) Prioritises a paradigmatic model (systems of choice/ options)
Demonstrate the universality and innateness of grammar	**Purpose**	Understand semantic variety and the relation between language, society and consciousness
No relation	**Relation to ideology**	Language is inherently ideological (SFL), or partially ideological (cognitive linguistics)

(continued)

Table 2.1 (continued)

Philosophical/psychological, formal strand Language as rule	Criteria	Ethnographic/sociological, functional strand Language as resource
No relation	**Relation to the social world**	Language construes and enacts the world and social relations
There is no connection beyond language being an innate capacity in the mind	**Relation to thought, consciousness, cognition**	Language shapes consciousness and higher cognitive functions
Language develops in the mind, as a 'pre-packaged set of structures' (Lukin 2019:12) SLA for second language learning Language Acquisition Device	**How language is learned**	Socio-constructivist Learned in interaction

The Philosophy/Psychology, 'Language as Rule' or 'Formal' Strand as a Dominant/Default Ontology

In the following section we explore the main ontological constructs of this strand and the critiques levelled at its application to language teaching. On this side of the ontological spectrum, we find 'formal linguistics' which tends to focus on syntax, clause level and sentence descriptions (such as verb form, tenses) and ways words are combined in sentences, and on semantics. The focus therefore is on syntagmatic relations, or the way words follow each other to form sentences, and focus on syntagmatic phenomenon such as subject-finite agreement, word order (this is a key difference with the functional systemic paradigmatic approach explained below). Bloomfield's American structuralism for example analysed phonology, morphology and some elements of syntax but paid little attention to semantics and had great impact on language teaching through audio-lingual approaches (Bloor & Bloor, 1996, p. 244). Traditional grammar has evolved from antiquity (Firth, 1957), and has had significant impact on language teaching. This approach to language theory aligns with the ontological constructs of the 'language as rule' strand, in particular its focus on syntax and clause-based description, its focus on accuracy, and its haphazard treatment of context and meaning.

This approach is pervasive in current pedagogical grammars and in common conceptions of language.

Although the 'philosophical' approach to language has a long history which precedes Chomsky (Halliday (2003), we have decided to focus on Chomsky's Transformative-Generative Grammar (TGG) as an illustration of this strand for the following reasons: Despite several of its concepts being contested, re-worked or abandoned over the years (and Chomsky himself expressing doubt about 'the significance, for the teaching of languages, of such [linguistic description] insights and understanding as have been attained in linguistics and psychology' (Chomsky, 1966/71, pp. 152–153)), TGG remains influential in terms of 'dominance and institutional power' (Matthiessen & Teruya, 2023), and in terms of implicit beliefs and practices about language. Beyond the rule focus that characterises this strand, TGG also contributed (or re-interpreted) several important concepts both in linguistics and language learning which have had a lasting influence on teaching practices. It is these implicit influences on language conceptions, directly inherited from TGG concepts or via theories it had a bearing on, such as Second Language Acquisition theories or pragmatics for example (see Hasan, 2011), which we want to discuss.

Briefly, the purpose of Chomskyan linguistics is to provide a scientific formalisation of all grammatical sentence structures as would be determined through a native speaker's intuition of accuracy and acceptability (Chomsky, 1957). The aim of the theory is to reveal innate and universal grammar rules. As is outlined in Table 2.1, core theoretical concepts include the **innate capacity for language** (the Language Acquisition Device), and its universality: language is genetically hard-wired through a language acquisition device (Sampson, 2005). Other very influential concepts are Chomsky's distinction between language **competence** (internal, and *ideal* knowledge of language, called i-language), and **performance** (use of language, e-language), mis-inherited from Saussure (Hasan, 2005). In TGG however, performance and meaning, are of no interest since they do not inform on the universal elements of language (Ellis, 1993). Performance is then picked up through additional frameworks such as pragmatics (Hasan, 2011). For Chomsky, linguistics is a branch of cognitive psychology and language is to be studied theoretically and out of its context of communication (2006, p. 1) and its user's position in the social context. In fact, for Chomsky, communication is not the function of language. The theory therefore does not account for any relation with the user, the context of use, the social world, or ideology (Lukin, 2019: ix). It also means thought is distinct from language, it precedes it (Lukin, 2019, p. 12). As Lukin explains, with this rejection of language in use as an object of study, TG is not equipped to answer any questions related to ideology (Lukin, 2019, p. 10), which is particularly concerning for those who aspire for social change through their educational practices.

The influence of these concepts is puzzling since linguists from a range of perspectives have critiqued TGG and the broader 'Language as rule' strand. For example, the notion that language is hard-wired in our brains is a claim for which there is no evidence (Sampson 2005; Hymes, 1964; Hagege, 1976; Seuren, 2004; Lakoff & Johnson, 1999, Halliday, 2003). Seargeant (2010) argues that Chomsky in fact *posits* rather than explores (or evidences) ontology (which is the intellectual equivalent of the '*Because I say so*' argument, only tenable thanks to significant symbolic capital- see below):

'From now on I will consider a language to be a set (finite or infinite) of sentences, each finite in length and constructed out of a finite set of elements. All natural languages in their spoken or written form are languages in this sense.'
Chomsky (1957, p.13)

The main problems are summarised in Butt (2019):

with Chomsky's work, syntax is presented as formal and autonomous; meaning is deferred and passed over to philosophy; the individual is the domain of study; the assumption of a genetically based universal grammar is used against any evidence of the 'typical actual' of language behaviour; a language is the collection of sentences generated by the formal rules of the language; and intuitions of grammaticality become the least assailable form of linguistic testimony.
Butt (2019, p. 5)

The focus on universals, and on native speakers' intuition for grammaticality have also made TG-influenced linguistics vulnerable to ethnocentricity since the basis for universal status is mostly drawn from English, or 'Standard Average European' (Whorf, in Halliday, 2003, p. 101). Ethnocentricity is evident in the Minimalist programme which argues that the word order SVO is universal (and when faced with counter-evidence from several languages, argues that those non SVO languages in fact function with an underlying SVO structure). The same baffling logic occurs in studies of colour terms across languages such as Berlin and Kay's (1969) very influential Basic Colour Terms Theory which devises and classifies languages into stages of development according to the number of colour terms found. Here too, English provides the ideal universal model: languages that do not appear to have terms for specific hues, nor even for 'color', are simply said to be developing, and to have 'semantic gaps' (Wierzicka, 2008).

Importantly Chomsky's separation between 'the study of the rule system of language from the study of the social rules which determine their contextual use' (Bernstein, 1971, p. 160) means 'Linguistics' is routinely dismissed as offering nothing useful to disciplines such as sociolinguistics and social sciences. Bourdieu and Wacquant (1992) for example reject TGG and Chomsky's sterile view of language, but in doing so, particularly in Bourdieu (1991), it is *all* linguistics that is rejected as having no relevance to the study of society and meaning. Bourdieu's conception of language is in fact far closer to the ethnographic/sociological strand (Ding & Monbec, 2024) but he seemed unaware of theories better aligned ontologically and better equipped to operationalise his sociological concepts (Hasan, 2005). Still today, too many in academia, social sciences, teacher education programmes, language teaching, and (embarrassingly) linguistics and sociolinguistics, equate the whole of linguistics with the psychology/philosophical, and Chomskyan ontological strand (Matthiessen & Teruya, 2023; Riemer, 2023).

There are several reasons that explain the dominance and continuing influence of this ontology. First, there is too little teaching of language ontology in schools, and in language teacher training. The belligerent attitude adopted to impose TG as the only linguistics available is also well documented (Harris, 1993/2021; Halliday, 2003). Harris' *The Linguistic Wars* (1993/2021), an anthropological analysis of the field in North America in the twentieth century reads like a soap opera, with its tribes, intrigues, strategising, falsehoods, dismissal, fights (a physical fight is reported, and plenty of shouting matches), appropriations, citation ghosting, and enmities. Koener (1983) argues the socio-political context including 'fashion', generous funding from the US Defence Department and favouristism from key journals (*Language*), as well as a glorifying rhetoric also bolstered the theory.

Beyond Chomsky's accumulated symbolic capital and power over the field, a key reason for this dominance, in our view, is that TGG is an a-historical, a-social and individual-based language ontology. By the very act of dissociating language from its social context, and ignoring the link between language, consciousness and world construal, it is particularly well suited to enable and perpetuate the mission of a neoliberal ruling system, in government and in education. Reimer (2023, p. 193) argues that formal linguistics training encourages a 'rule-governed, hierarchical and dispassionate decision-making norms that are essential to the ideology of contemporary bureaucratic administration'. A language ontology which links language with society opens up the possibility to ask why language is being used the way it is. The minefield which is the literacy field (discussed in Part 2) attests to the high political and ideological stakes implicit in these ontological alignments.

A Functional Ontology, an Appliable Linguistics

'Linguistics cannot be other than an ideologically committed form of social action'
Halliday (1985, p. 5).

This quote (well known to Systemicists) sets a clear contrast with the previous paragraphs. The twentieth century saw the development of significant ethno/socio/cognitive linguistics theories such as Systemic Functional Semiotics, Cognitive Linguistics (Lakoff, 1980), Ecolinguistics (Halliday is credited with coining the term in 1992, then further developed, see Stibbe, 2021), which focused on meaning and real-world application. In this section we focus on SFL, a social semiotics model of language developed by Michael Halliday, and colleagues, which draws from Saussure, Hjelmslev, Malinowski, Whorf and Firth (for a brief overview of this heritage, see Martin, 2016). Michael Halliday's work in social semiotics began in the Chinese language classroom to address the language teaching problems he encountered. SFL has since expanded into an elaborate theoretical framework that has maintained its 'appliable' purpose of solving theoretical and practical language-related issues (Halliday, 2006, in Martin, 2013, p. 189), being used in a wide variety of fields such as translation, computational linguistics, healthcare, education. Appliability is a major characteristic: the dialectic between theory and practice is integral to the theory. In this section we simply high-light the fundamental repercussions its key ontological constructs listed in Table 2.1 have for educational practice.[2]

SFL is **a social theory of language**; it theorises language as a **meaning-making social semiotics resource**, from which users choose according to their context of communication. Language is *always* studied in relation to meaning and the social world.

A note to the reader, if the following few paragraphs appear a little abstract, part 2 of this chapter details the concrete implications for teaching approaches and policy. Chapter 6 details what these ontological concepts mean in teaching practice. However, it is through an understanding of the ontological perspectives that flexible application can be done in classroom, so the following knowledge is important for the practitioner.

Construal and **enactment** refer to the deep connection between human experience and the inner structure of language. **Construal** is a key notion, and highlights language as the 'principle means through which we create the world in which we live' (Halliday, 2003, p. 114), and its role in shaping our understanding of the world (Lukin, 2019, p.17). To say that language construes the world and enacts relationships means it provides the main frames for our worldview, it makes some elements, ideas, agents, salient and erases others. This positions SFL closely to the linguistics rela-tivity/Sapir-Whorf hypothesis on language and thought, where language is seen as mediating the world and shaping consciousness, or the way the world is categorised and understood. Taking the example of colour terms once more, Wierzbicka (2008) argues that when terms such as red, green or blue, or the term *colour* itself, do not exist in a language as is the case in Warlpiri, one of the largest Aboriginal languages in Australia, the concepts do not exist in minds either. In SFL, the link between language and consciousness is inextricable and this also means that ideology is an inescapably inherent part of language (Lukin, 2019, p. 16; Hasan, 2005).

Language is 'not only a way of thinking about the world; it is also, at one and the same time, a way of acting on the world – which means, of course, acting on the other people in it' (Halliday, 1992, p. 384). Along with construing experience, **enacting** or 'acting out the interper-sonal encounters' (Halliday, 2003) means we use language to set up and maintain relationships, dialogues, according to our values, and beliefs, and

---

[2] For an SFL bibliography, see Monbec (2022).

according to power and status differential among participants (Halliday, 2003, p. 16). Social groups are organised and value systems reproduced indirectly, 'though the accumulated experience of numerous small events, insignificant in themselves [...] it is in the most ordinary everyday uses of language with parents, brothers and sisters, neighborhood children, in the home, on the street...[...] that serves to transmit, to the child, the essential qualities of the society and the nature of social being' (Halliday 1974, p. 4, as cited in Hasan, 1996, p. 26). In this way, SFL is particularly well suited to support social theories such as Bernstein's code theory which aims to explain how subjects' positioning impacts their orientation to meaning and their discourse (Hasan, 2005).

A Stratified and Metafunctional Architecture Suited to Teaching: SFL is a theory of language, not just lexicogrammar, it includes discourse semantics (Martin, 1992), lexicogrammar (Halliday & Matthiessen, 2013) and phonology/ graphology (Halliday & Greaves, 2008). Because it is a social theory of language, it also theorises social context as register and genre (Martin, 1992; Martin & Rose, 2008). The relation between these strata (and so between the social world and language) are also theorised through concepts such as realisation, instantiation and individuation. Key elements in SFL linguistics description are its distinction between syntagms (sequences of class), and structures (configuration of functions), allowing for form to represent different functions, and function to be realised as a variety of forms. SFL prioritises *paradigmatic* relations (rather than syntagmatic) and represents description as systems of functions (rather than trees of class), which allows it to map language as meaning potential (rather than rules and sequences). In other words, SFL organises language *paradigmatically*, as choice, rather than sequence. So, instead of focusing on sequential relations (syntagmatic)—what comes after what as in: *If + I + finish + this + chapter + today)*, SFL focuses on what can come *instead (paradigmatic)*, what resource constitutes an alternative selection, and so an alternative meaning. A system, then is a set of paradigmatic choices (Bloor & Bloor, 1995). This directly links to another ontological distinction in SFL, which is its theorising of meaning, through its description of broad language/semiotics ideational, textual and interpersonal **metafunctions**. SFL describes context through register variables of field (the topic), mode (the means of communication) and tenor (the power relations, positioning and evaluations). These variables are then (respectively) construed, composed, and enacted by ideational, textual and interpersonal semiotic resources (Martin, 2016).

Language learning is also viewed differently within this ontological strand. For Halliday, common metaphors used in the philosophy/psychology strand such as 'acquisition' presents language as a commodity. For Halliday (2004 [1978], p. 37): 'A child's construction of language is at once both a part of and a means of his construction of reality; and it is natural to Western thinking to view both these processes largely from the standpoint of the individual'. In this, Halliday and SFL are closely related to social constructivists and in particular Vygotsky who sees language learning as a construction that occurs through interaction with members of the culture and views higher order mental functions as developing with language (Vygotsky, 2011). This sociocultural linguistic approach to language and learning contrasts with a view that linguistic competence is innate and purely cognitive. In social semiotics (and social constructivism), language is at the heart of teaching and learning processes, language is not just an object of study, it is the mediator through which we learn (Byrnes, 2009; Coffin & Donohue, 2014). In his language-based theory of learning, Halliday (2004) refers to *Learning language* (learning to use language), *Learning about language* (learn how to put language together to communicate) and *Learning through language* (learning about the world, including disciplinary knowledge).

The Systemic Functional Linguistics theory overviewed here has informed language teaching over decades in many educational contexts. The Sydney School Genre Pedagogy, for example, has been applied widely. Yet, in some incarnation, the approach might still be limited by the fact that the concepts that are key to its ontological distinction might be given less importance than its lexicogrammatical descriptions. In Chapter 4, we discuss the social justice claims and aspirations inherent to SFL/Genre pedagogy.

THE LANGUAGE ILLUSIO IMPACT

Having established a few core constructs around language ontology in the previous section, we now focus on the impact a lack of attention to language ontology may have, both on mis-framing and misunderstanding language-related issues and on generating solutions that underwhelm or miss the mark. We use this ontological lens to review the broad discursive climate around language, and to discuss ideologies around notions such as ideal competence and native speakerism, literacy teaching and the misunderstanding of the nature of academic discourse. We also consider ontological assumptions in practices such as needs analysis, curriculum and assessment design and the teaching of grammar, many of which deserve an un-dogmatic rethink.

Clarifying the Discourse Around Language in Literacy Policy and Linguistics-Informed Language Teaching

In the UK educational context, the teaching of language (Literacy, Foreign Languages, or EAL) has generated intense debates, acerbated by a focus on school results and inspections by bodies like the Office for Standards in Education, Children's Services and Skills (OFSTED), and amplified by a mass media and public discourse that exploit the political dimension and divisive potential of language and literacy at the cost of a complex and nuanced conversation. This is important for our argument because higher education language practitioners, academics across campus, and the general population are steeped in these discourses and understandings, and might enact them in their educational practices, or reify them even as they resist them. The complexity and murkiness can partly be attributed to the conflation of different ontologies of language, and different definitions of grammar and literacy. Public discourse about language seems to be skewed towards a formal ontology, with discussions of standards, and norms taken for granted, often endorsed, sometimes vilified, but rarely ontologically critiqued. It often exhibits a lack of understanding of the nature of language and its power. Over the last decades in England, there has been a struggle over approaches to literacy and language teaching in schools that seem to pit language as rule vs language as resource. In the 1960s, functional literacy teaching materials were pioneered by Michael Halliday who provided a radical break from traditional rule-based language teaching (Acevedo, 2020, p. 5). In the 1980s, Halliday's influence was still evident through materials that focused on meaning-making and conscious attention to the way language functions (the Kingman Report, 1988). Meanwhile, the teaching of language as rule has often been dismissed as too prescriptive, through progressive notions of 'learner-centeredness' or psychological perspectives on child development. This rejection ostentatiously targets a formal ontology, and practices such as grammar rule teaching, labelling of parts of speech, and pronunciation drills, which are portrayed as irrelevant and elitist. While the 'language as resource' ontology is less often overtly targeted (because it is absent or invisible), this broad-brush dismissal of knowledge about language, means a functional 'language as resource' ontology suffers the same repudiation. In the 1990s a multimillion-pound development of materials based on a functional approach and a social theory of language was shelved by the UK government. The head of the programme had an insightful analysis of why this happened:

> The emphasis on language variation and on language in context led to a too frequent reference to social theory and an emphasis on sociolinguistic perspectives. For governments of a particular political persuasion the word social is directly equitable with the word socialist... The government eventually made it clear that it had preferred all along training materials which emphasised right and wrong uses of English, reinforcing such an emphasis with drills and exercises for teachers and pupils to follow, and with a printed appendix containing the correct answers to the exercises.
> (Carter, 1997, p. 44 in Acevedo, 2020).

Aided by media and common sense understanding of language, the initiative was thwarted, the discourse around it muddled and the potential of language for social change was buried deep under notions of 'back to basics', and a re-working of an SFL/Genre approach into an uncritical recipe for writing which led to genre pedagogy being rejected in the UK (see Acevedo, 2020, for a full history of these struggles over literacy and language teaching).

Moving beyond these acrimonious debates requires ontological clarity and the ability to encompass different views and nuanced arguments. Teaching language as a set of disconnected rules is not terribly useful, nor inspiring. Yet, within a functional approach, formal accuracy can be taught critically as part of the dominant register, itself acknowledged as a social and political construct, with a view to empower students. Furthermore, all repertoires and manners of speaking and writing are equal in intrinsic value, and it is wrong to view non-standard individual repertoires as inferior. Yet linguistic discrimination is a real phenomenon with concrete consequences on students' lives and prospects, and mastery of certain prestigious registers impact how speakers' status, educational level or even cognitive abilities are perceived (finding this fact abhorrent makes it no less true) and so giving critical access to a range of registers to *all* students is essential. The ability to notice, to access and use (or not) the dominant register (however we want to call this) has an impact on agency (Hasan, 1996).

A serious issue however is that the occasional initiatives that aim to boost a linguistics-informed approach to language teaching are rarely clear about ontology, often using the term 'linguistics' without any further qualification and so, often, adopting a version of the dominant ontology. This leaves these initiatives vulnerable to criticism, and approaches that cast formal linguistics as a novel and exciting notion in language teaching are/have been destined to indifference at bests limited in their ability to instil passion about the wonder and power of language and meaning-making, to address teaching and learning issues and to provide transformational potential.

In these recurring swings of the pendulum between conservative and progressive ideas about language, the covert victim is *functional knowledge* which is erased from view. This cuts us off from an understanding of language as a tool for both world and consciousness shaping and so, as Hasan argues, it forecloses the ability to 'examine the very reality created by it' (1996, p. 34). Disappearing knowledge about language is a socio-political issue; it impacts students' access to a range of registers and directly limits their agency in different social contexts (we discuss this further in Chapter 4).

Competence and the Deficit View of Language

When language knowledge is erased, dismissed or belittled, barren curriculum space can be claimed by more tangential elements such as autonomy, independent-learning, confidence, reflectivity and cultural awareness (which is not to say these are not important). Syllabi can also start looking like haphazard lists of skills: Reading skills, for example, reduced to practices of questionable relevance such as 'skimming' and 'scanning', which have the effect of both characterising reading as a frantic search for information (which it is not, especially not in higher education) and to occlude crucial close reading practices which require the language knowledge necessary to engage deeply in the ideas and thinking of others (Monbec, 2024).

Even when language is the focus of practices, ontology plays tricks. Whether educators align explicitly with a formal view or not, the notion of *ideal* linguistic **competence** seems to be pervasive. Competence is—like language—polysemous and ambiguous (Anderson, 2023). For Chomsky, competence is the perfect, idealised and implicit language knowledge of the ideal (native) speaker (1965, p. 3), which Anderson (2023) argues, remains the most influential understanding of the term in Applied Linguistics. Other definitions, such as Hymes' (1972) have incorporated notions of communication (taken up in Communicative approach to language teaching), but Anderson shows that while the term competence is often associated with Hymes (1972), theoretical underpinning remains within 'the grammar-focused, integrationist, native-speakerist Chomskyan tradition' (2023, p. 9).

The notion of competence is directly implicated in language ideology and a deficit view of language. To posit an ideal form of language embodied by an ideal speaker marks out those who do not produce it (whether L1 or L2 speakers) and allows the concept of 'standard' to be seen as a natural state of things, rather than a socially and politically constructed notion and a tool of social reproduction. This applies to students who do not have the language of instruction as mother tongue but also to those who are less familiar with academic prose (according to various criteria, many of which very subjective, and poorly measured). The deficit view is this habit of noticing language when it is 'wrong' rather than for what and how it *means*, and it reverberates through educational practices across disciplines. It also seeps through common sense knowledge about language which explains why so often, the term language collocates with evaluative terms such as good, bad, poor, wrong and (in)correct. When we view 'standard' norms rather than 'registers' as the object of our teaching, we get into all sorts of difficulties and contradictions from needs analysis to syllabus design, assessment and the teaching of 'grammar', which need to be unpacked:

Needs analysis: we do not think it is possible to have an a-theoretical (or a-ontological) approach to needs analysis: in other words, we do not approach student needs or their academic context of communication without pre-existing ontological assumptions about language. Unpacking our own ontological orientations as we analyse student needs is the only way to counteract the illusion that we are approaching needs analysis as clean slates. In the same way, CURRICULUM, syllabus and materials design cannot be dissociated from ontological assumptions which directly affect what is selected as teaching content, whether the syllabus is organised around language 'points' and rules, a prioritisation of verb forms, or as bundles of resources that realise specific meanings, include connection to context and reference to meanings beyond the clause. Key manifestations of an alignment with a default formal ontology in syllabus design, assessment and pedagogy may include the teaching of language features as isolated and decontextualised (which means no reference to broader context, nor co-text), a focus on sentence level syntax rather than discourse features across texts (which means a lack of attention to patterns across texts), a lack of connection to an overall architecture of meanings, or rhetorical purpose (in terms of context, purpose, audience); a tendency to see uncritiqued normative standards as the object of teaching, and teaching the arbitrary as natural. Genre-based approaches so common in EAP (mostly through ESP or SFL/Genre) vary quite significantly in terms of language ontology and this is reflected in how they address meaning resources at discourse semantic and lexicogrammatical level, and how they relate this to contextual features. In conversations between colleagues, ontological assumptions also subtly show through semantic shifts with terms such as 'competence' as seen above, or even conflation between terms like 'grammar' and 'accuracy' or 'pronunciation' and 'received pronunciation'. The term language itself is polysemous, and when it is used to mean 'grammatical accuracy at sentence level' in discussions around the place of *language* in syllabus, this leads to conversations at cross purposes with more functional-oriented colleagues who see most of what they do as 'language'.

Assessment practices are not exempt: analytical rubrics that separate 'language' away from content and organisation (most of them do) clearly do not see language as a resource that realises content (field), organisation (mode) and evaluation (tenor). However, the concept of 'organisation' is realised through a range of generic stages, discourse semantics systems such as identification (the tracking of people, places and things), and periodicity (rhythm of discourse, signposts and consolidation), involving Theme and New, Macro and hyperThemes, thematic progression and lexicogrammar resources such as lexical chains, reference and deictic, and general nouns. Rubrics where 'language' is kept apart, equated to accuracy or ill-defined notions like appropriacy or style, ignore the intrinsic relevance of language to every criteria of the rubric: content should include and evaluate the linguistic resources that express and critique content, while organisation should be explicit about the semiotic resources that organise the text (Monbec et al., 2021).

Finally, due to the lack of shared definition of the term, the teaching of 'grammar' is often conflated with the teaching of accuracy, conventions or standard forms. Pedagogical grammars, and grammar textbooks which have shaped many educators' understandings of language and their practice, say little, if anything, about language ontology and tend to accept a 'cannon of pedagogical grammar [..] unquestioningly' (Burton, 2019, p. 4) organised around lists of 'language points'. In teacher development resources, some of which are cornerstones in ELT and EAP language teacher training, discussions tend to cover what type of language is to be modelled (whether it is data-driven and authentic or made-up), whether grammar should be taught explicitly or not, what is good (academic) language, or what is good grammar, but ontological questions seem foreclosed, almost made invisible in the language teaching discourse, meaning the question is occluded from the beginning of a teacher's development. This is particularly important to address because the canon shapes reading lists in teacher training programmes and reproduces the same narrow and problematic knowledge base. A deficit view of language has serious consequences on the field, playing a significant role in marginalising language provisions and their practitioners as language fixers.

Native Speakerism (the Zombie-Like Return of)

The 'ideal competence' discussed above is also linked with ideologies such as **native speakerism,** and here again, we argue that going back to ontology helps us understand the perpetuation of certain ideologies. Native speakerism has generated a large body of literature over decades without any signs of abatement. In this section, we argue that part of this zombie-like return of the NS ideology in the field is related to poor ontological understanding of language. Braine (1999), prompted by what he observed in ELT in Hong Kong, showed how the concept shaped the construction of the legitimate teacher, the legitimate expert as native speaker, often monolingual. Explained convincingly through colonialism and imperialism (Pennycook, 1994; Philipson, 1992; O'Regan, 2021), native speakerism might appear to be *only* a matter of political history and economic domination. Tupas (2022), for example, shows how coloniality enabled native speakerism, but argues that 'any perspective on ways to combat hegemonic discourses and practices in the use, teaching and learning of English remains hugely inadequate if its solutions stay on the level of the "linguistic" and the "cultural" and ignore the role of structures of colonialism and globalization'. While we understand the focus of Tupas' research and agree with the point he is making, this sentence, also exemplifies the ontological ambiguousness we find pervasive in sociolinguistics: it gives the impression that linguistics is monolithic, that it is already being used to solve the issue and that it is not adequate. If it is a 'language as rule' ontology Tupas is dismissing, we agree that a thorough critique is indeed necessary, but we argue that, on the contrary, linguistics from a functional, 'language as resource' ontology has hardly begun to be explored for its potential to address discourse hegemony, agents positioning and legitimation strategies in language teaching provisions. When Tupas suggests that 'Teacher education programs informed by various iterations of paradigms of Global Englishes must be reconfigured in such a way that race and colonial history take the centre stage in the education of teachers and students of English' (2022, p.11), we fear that without also including a serious attention to the way these power structures are kept in place over and over through an unquestioned alignment to a 'language as rule' ontology, these suggested reconfigurations might lack substance and power.

In our view, native speakerism can only thrive on an unspoken language ontology built on concepts such as 'ideal competence' which conflate the legitimate knower with the native speaker. With this ideal competence and focus on the universal and innate ability, the learner (including the colonised or linguistically deficient, after Pennycook) cannot be built in any other way but as in a linguistic deficit position. An ontology that conceptualises language as an asocial, apolitical entity modelled on a standard ideal speaker construct is the essence of any linguistic imperialism or classist endeavour. Within a functional ontology, the notion of ideal competence does not exist theoretically, only as a sociological concept which can be critiqued if language is taught in terms of variety, registers and repertoire.

Language Learning Approaches

Despite recent moves towards more sociocultural, multilingual and inclusive approaches to language learning, the field has traditionally been characterised by an uneasy relation with language ontology (see Ellis, 2021 for a historical overview of the field). This is most obvious in a tendency to dismiss knowledge about language as harmful to language learning processes (an example of this is Freedman's 1993 well known critique of explicit knowledge in genre pedagogy, which is labelled useless or harmful—a strong claim which is based on 6 law students). A related tendency is to classify knowledge into false dichotomies such as procedural vs declarative knowledge (these are actually forms of kno*wing*) which are then used to dismiss knowledge about language altogether. In educational settings, accessing procedural ways of knowing is amply aided by declarative knowing (if by this we mean visible functional knowledge about language and meaning-making). Second Language Acquisition approaches have traditionally shown a preference for designing natural interactions to support students' innate cognitive capacity for language acquisition (Anderson, 2023). As Anderson (2022) argues, Chomsky's 'acquisition model' for early childhood language learning (1965, p. 30) was embraced in SLA and much of it hinged around the ideal and innate competence and language conceptualised in terms of rules to be sequenced and acquired. This alignment led to hypotheses such as Acquisition-Learning, the Natural Order, the Monitor, the Input, the Affective Filter hypotheses, all rife with ontological assumptions and led to pedagogical models that favour assimilation or integration to a norm (Anderson, 2023). It might be the case that some language teaching programmes now propose balanced critiques but as Gass, Benhney and Plonsky (2020, p. 128) explain, while Krashen's model has been shown as 'vacuous', 'his work lives on in much of what we know today about second language learning'. To take a few examples, the Contrasting Analysis Hypothesis (which links first language with errors made in the learnt language) has been partially discredited in its different iterations but still remains influential in pedagogical materials according to Burton (2019). The Critical-Period hypothesis with its claim that an early start in second language learning ensures better fluency and phonological assimilation might be invalidated (Singleton & Muñoz, 2011) and critiqued for placing the 'native competency' as a goal of language learning (Kubota, 2015), but it still informs policy such as unquestioned expansion of English language teaching in primary school contexts. Educational practices like the monolingualism fallacy, realised in classrooms through policies like 'No L1 in the classroom' (overtly to maximise practice in the target language, but in essence possibly to protect monolingual Anglophone teachers' legitimacy) might be starting to wane in some contexts (Renandya et al., 2023; Tupas & Renandya, 2021) but remain current in others (Le Chen, 2020). The strong SLA focus on learners' psychological traits such as motivation, affect, extroversion or grit also needs to be examined, for its tendency to be associated with cultural stereotyping, but also for preventing educators from critically evaluating their curriculum content (Monbec, 2019), i.e. there might be a more reflective conclusion to be drawn from poor student engagement than to blame students' motivation. The above paragraph makes broad claims due to space, and may not apply to all readers' contexts nor describe all readers' experience, yet these are field-level orientations which continue to shape, in many ways implicitely, the legitimate agent, legitimate knowledge, and practices.

Access to Academic Language and Academic Writing

Ontological clarification would also benefit discussions of access to academic discourse/writing. Students' challenges with academic writing are often blamed on and conflated with a dismissal of academic discourse around its density, opaqueness, and eliteness. The issue deserves a more careful discussion than is often afforded. First, the reasons advanced for this density and opaqueness are often incorrect: density is not necessarily due to pompousness or affectation, density is not always avoidable. Most importantly, academic language is not (just) about arbitrary conventions (and when we do encounter arbitrary conventions, we should discuss them as such, leaving it to students to flout them when they feel they can).

For Halliday, and within SFL ontology, '[l]anguage is as it is because of the functions it has evolved to serve in people's lives' (Halliday, 1978, pp. 3–4). Halliday produced an ontogenesis of scientific discourse from the fourteenth century to the present that studied the evolution of lexicogrammar in scientific texts (2016). He traced the emergence of features of the grammar, including grammatical metaphor, nominalisations, technical terms used as general nouns, deictic for texture and organisation of larger patterns across texts, as language evolved to serve the specific semiotic needs of scientific knowledge creation. These features evolved to reflect specific epistemologies and suited the construction of knowledge occurring at the time and in this respect, they are 'not merely arbitrary conventions' (Halliday, 2016, p. 18). As the functional ontology of language sees ideology as an integral part of language, it is also true that this language evolution supports a certain worldview and should be open to critique as these features are an integral part of educational, political and media discourse. However, when we conflate the evolution of a dense and technical semiotic resource with 'superfluousness', we miss the real difference between meaning-rich academic discourse and obscure, dense but meaning-light prose (Maton, 2013). While the first conveys rich, complex and technical knowledge (that might require several rounds of close reading), the other is akin to what we can all recognise as empty managerial discourse (which cannot receive the criticism it deserves without appropriate knowledge of language ontology). While both discourses should be opened to critique, they are not the same at all.

Uninformed critiques and poorly understood problems can then lead to *non sequitur* solutions. For example, those who dismiss academic discourse might claim that school genres should be replaced by non-academic genres (such as personal stories or comics). This is problematic. First, any awareness of a functional language ontology makes clear the intimate relation between genre and linguistic resources with meaning-making potential: one can write a thesis through a comic (it has been done), but the knowledge communicated is not the same. More importantly, suggesting that non-academic genres are more accessible to students traditionally excluded is not only condescending, it also completely ignores these genres' specific complexity. It is not less difficult to write a comic or a blog than to write a report or an essay: the genre specificities and the assessment criteria still need to be made visible to students. Regardless of the genre, it is awareness of the linguistic and multimodal meaning-making demands entailed that are paramount for access and success. Changing assignment genres, invoking creativity, in the name of inclusivity and access, but without making the basis of achievement visible is very problematic. Diversifying genres in schools and higher education is to be encouraged (and is happening!) but deserves very careful implementation.

Conclusion

This second chapter has provided an overview of ontological orientations to language which inform educational practices, discourse and policy. The chapter has discussed persisting language ideologies, doxic values and beliefs from an ontological perspective. We hope it has provided tools to bring language ontology to the forefront of educational reflections, to better understand current discourse and threats around language provision, and to enrich practices.

References

Accurso, K. (2019). *Learning linguistics, teaching for change: Preparing secondary educators to more equitably teach disciplinary literacies*. PhD Thesis. University of Massachusetts Amherst.

Acevedo, M. C. (2020). *Bringing language to consciousness: Teacher professional learning in genre-based reading pedagogy.* PhD Thesis. Open University (United Kingdom).

Alvarro, J. (2014). 中國英文報紙中的意識形態語言: *The language of ideology in China's English press: Representations of dissent.* Doctoral dissertation. City University of Hong Kong.

Anderson, J. (2022). What's in a name? Why 'SLA' is no longer fit for purpose and the emerging, more equitable alternatives. *Language Teaching, 55,* 427–433.

Anderson, J. (2023). Reimagining educational linguistics: A post-competence perspective. *Educational Linguistics.* https://doi.org/10.1515/eduling-2023-0009

Berlin, B., & Kay, P. (1969). *Basic color terms: Their universality and evolution.* University of California Press.

Bernstein, B. (1971). *Class, codes and control.* Routledge & Kegan Paul.

Blackburn, S. (1995). History of the philosophy of language. In T. Honderich (Ed.), *Oxford companion to philosophy.* Oxford University Press.

Bloor, T., & Bloor, M. (1996). *The functional analysis of English: A Hallidayan approach.* Arnold.

Bourdieu, P. (1991). *Language and symbolic power.* Harvard University Press.

Bourdieu, P., & Wacquant, L. (1992). *An invitation to reflexive sociology.* Polity Press.

Braine, G. (1999). From the periphery to the centre: One teacher's journey. In G. Braine (Ed.), *Non-native educators in English language teaching* (pp. 15–39). Lawrence Erlbaum Associates.

Burton, G. F. (2019). *The canon of pedagogical grammar for ELT—A mixed methods study of its evolution, development and comparison with evidence on learner output.* PhD Thesis. University of Limerick.

Butt, D. (2019). The 'history of ideas' and Halliday's natural science of meaning. In M. A. K. Halliday & J. J. Webster (Eds.), *Bloomsbury companion to systemic functional linguistics* (pp. 45–62). Bloomsbury.

Byrnes, H. (2009). Systemic-functional reflections on instructed foreign language acquisition as meaning-making: An introduction. *The Modern Language Journal, 20,* 1–9.

Canut, C., Guellouz, M., & Makoni, S. (2022). Sinfree Makoni: Pour une nouvelle ontologie du langage. *Semen. Revue De Sémio-Linguistique des Textes Et Discours, 50*(2), 117–133.

Chen, L. (2020). Problematising the English-only policy in EAP: A mixed-methods investigation of Chinese international students' perspectives of academic language policy. *Journal of Multilingual and Multicultural Development, 41*(8), 718–735. https://doi.org/10.1080/01434632.2019.1643355

Chomsky, N. (1957). Logical structure in language. *Journal of the American Society for Information Science, 8*(4), 284.

Chomsky, N. (1965). *Aspects of the theory of syntax*. MIT Press.

Chomsky, N. (1966). Linguistic theory. In R. G. Mead (Ed.), *Language teaching: Broader contexts* (pp. 93–112). Northeast conference on the teaching of modern languages: Reports of the working committees. MLA Materials Center.

Chomsky, N. (2006). *Language and mind*. Cambridge University Press.

Coffin, C., & Donohue, J. (2014). *A language as social semiotic-based approach to teaching and learning in higher education*. Wiley.

DELTA Syllabus Specifications. (2022). Cambridge University Press & Assessment. https://www.cambridgeenglish.org/Images/22096-delta-syllabus.pdf

Ding, A., & Bruce, I. (2017). *The English for academic purposes practitioner: Operating on the edge of academia*. Palgrave Macmillan.

Ding, A., & Monbec, L. (2024). A socio-analysis of English for academic purposes. In A. Ding & L. Monbec (Eds.), *Practitioner agency and identity in English for academic purposes*. Bloomsbury.

Ellis, J. (1993). *Language, thought, and logic*. Northwestern University Press.

Ellis, R. (2021). A short history of SLA: Where have we come from and where are we going? *Language Teaching, 54*(2), 190–205. https://doi.org/10.1017/S0261444820000038

Firth, J. R. (1957). *Papers in linguistics 1934–1951*. Oxford University Press.

Gass, S. M., Behney, J., & Plonsky, L. (2020). *Second language acquisition: An introductory course* (5th ed.). Routledge.

Hagege, C. (1976). *La grammaire generative: Réflexions critiques*. Presses Universitaires de France.

Hall, G., & Wicaksono, R. (Eds.). (2020). *Ontologies of English*. Cambridge University Press.

Halliday, M. A. K. (1974). *Language and Social Man*. London: Longman.

Halliday, M. A. K. (1978). *Language as social semiotic: The social interpretation of language and meaning*. Edward Arnold.

Halliday, M. A. K. (1985). *An introduction to functional grammar*. Edward Arnold.

Halliday, M. A. (1992). New ways of meaning: The challenge to applied linguistics. In M. Putz (Ed.), *Thirty years of linguistic evolution* (pp. 59–95).

Halliday, M. A. K. (2003). On language and linguistics: Volume 3 in the collected works of M.A.K. Halliday. In J. J. Webster (Ed.), *The collected works of M.A.K. Halliday* (pp. 1–15). Continuum.

Halliday, M. A. K., & Matthiessen, C. M. I. M. (2013). *Halliday's introduction to functional grammar* (4th ed.). Routledge.

Halliday, M. A. K., & Greaves, W. S. (2008). *Intonation in the grammar of English*. Equinox.

Harris, R. A. (1993/2021). *The linguistics wars*. Oxford University Press.
Hasan, R. (1996). *Ways of saying: Ways of meaning (C. Cloran, D. Butt, & G. Williams, Eds.)*. Cassell.
Hasan, R. (2011). A view of pragmatics in a social semiotic perspective. *Linguistics & the Human Sciences, 5*(3), 183–212.
Hasan, R. (2011). *Language and education: Learning and teaching in society* (Vol. 3). In J. Webster (Ed.) The Collected Works of Ruqaiya Hasan. Equinox. London: Equinox.
Hasan, R. (2005). Language, Society and Consciousness (Vol. 1). In J. Webster (Ed.). *The Collected Works of Ruqaiya Hasan*. Equinox.
Hymes, D. (1964). Introduction: Toward ethnographies of communication 1. *American Anthropologist, 66*(6_PART2), 1–34.
Hymes, D. (1972). On communicative competence. In J. B. Pride & J. Holmes (Eds.), *Sociolinguistics: Selected readings* (pp. 269–293). Penguin.
Klein, N. (2023). *Doppelganger: A trip into the mirror world*. Knopf Canada.
Klemperer, V. (2006). *Language of the Third Reich: LTI: Lingua Tertii Imperii*. A&C Black.
Koerner, K. (1983). The Chomskyan 'revolution' and its historiography: A few critical remarks. *Language & Communication, 3*(2), 147–169.
Kubota, R. (2015). Questioning language myths in English language teaching: Toward border-crossing communication. In *Selected papers from the twenty-fourth international symposium on English teaching* (pp. 44–57). English Teachers' Association-Republic of China (ETA-ROC).
Lakoff, G., & Johnson, M. (1980). *Metaphors we live by*. University of Chicago Press.
Lakoff, G., & Johnson, M. (1999). *Philosophy in the flesh: The embodied mind and its challenge to Western thought*. Basic Books.
Lukin, A. (2019). *War and its ideologies*. Springer.
Martin, J. R. (1982). Review of G. Sampson's School of Linguistics. *Australian Journal of Linguistics. 2* (1), 97–115.
Martin, J. R. (1992). *English text: System and structure*. John Benjamins.
Martin, J. R. (2016). Meaning matters: A short history of systemic functional linguistics. *WORD, 62*(1), 35–58. https://doi.org/10.1080/004 37956.2016.1141939
Martin, J. R., & Rose, D. (2008). *Genre relations: Mapping culture*. Equinox.
Martin, J. R., Doran, Y. J., & Figueredo, G. (Eds.). (2020). *Systemic functional language description: Making meaning matter*. Routledge.
Maton, K. (2013). *Knowledge and knowers: Towards a realist sociology of education*. Routledge.
Matthiessen, C. M. I. M., & Teruya, K. (2023). *Systemic functional linguistics: A complete guide*. Taylor & Francis.

Monbec, L. (2019). *Transfer from English for academic purposes to disciplinary modules*. EdD Thesis. Open University (United Kingdom).

Monbec, L., Tilakaratna, N., Brooke, M., Siew, T. L., Chan, Y. S., & Wu, V. (2021). Designing a rubric for reflection in nursing: A legitimation code theory and systemic functional linguistics-informed framework. *Assessment & Evaluation in Higher Education*. https://doi.org/10.1080/02602938.2020.1855414

Monbec, L. (2022). *Systemic functional linguistics for the self-taught*. BALEAP Research and Publications.

Monbec, L. (2024). Understanding students' reflective engagement with academic texts. In N. Tilakaratna & E. Szenes (Eds.) *Demystifying Critical Reflection: Improving pedagogy and practice with Legitimation Code Theory* (pp. 228–247). Routledge.

O'Regan, J. P. (2021). *Global English and political economy*. Routledge.

Pennycook, A. (1994). *The cultural politics of English as an international language*. Longman.

Phillipson, R. (1992). *Linguistic imperialism*. Oxford University Press.

Reimer, N. (2023). Domination and underlying form in linguistics. In A. Kaiper-Marquez, V. Milojičić, C. Severo, & A. Abdelhay (Eds.), *Shades of decolonial voices in linguistics* (pp. 45–60). Multilingual Matters.

Renandya, W. A., Nguyen, T. T. M., & Jacobs, G. M. (2023). Learning to unlearn faulty beliefs and practices in English language teaching. *Studies in English Language and Education, 10*(1), 1–15. https://doi.org/10.24815/siele.v10i1.26009

Robbins, R. H. (2013). *A short history of linguistics* (4th ed.). Routledge.

Sampson, G. (1980). *Schools of linguistics: Competition and evolution*. Hutchinson.

Sampson, G. (2005). *The 'Language Instinct' Debate*. A&C Black.

Seargeant, P. (2009). *Language ideology, language theory, and the regulation of linguistic behaviour. Language Sciences, 31*(4), 345–359.

Seargeant, P. (2010). The historical ontology of language. *Language Sciences, 32*(1), 1–13.

Seuren, P. A. (2004). *Chomsky's minimalism*. Oxford University Press.

Singleton, D., & Muñoz, C. (2011). Around and beyond the critical period hypothesis. In E. Hinkle (Ed.), *Handbook of research in second language teaching and learning* (pp. 407–425). Routledge.

Snyder, T. (2017). *On tyranny: Twenty lessons from the twentieth century*. Tim Duggan Books.

Stibbe, A. (2021). *Ecolinguistics: Language, ecology and the stories we live by* (2nd ed.). Routledge.

Szenes, E. (2021). Neo-Nazi environmentalism: The linguistic construction of ecofascism in a Nordic Resistance Movement manifesto. *Journal for Deradicalization, 27*, 146–192.

Tupas, R. (2022). The coloniality of native speakerism. *Asian Englishes*. https://doi.org/10.1080/13488678.2022.2056797

Tupas, R., & Renandya, W. A. (2021). Unequal Englishes: Re-envisioning the teaching of English in linguistically diverse classrooms. In B. Spolsky & H. Lee (Eds.), *Localizing global English: Asian perspectives and practices* (pp. 47–62). Routledge.

Vygotsky, L. S. (2011). *Thought and language* (E. Hanfmann, G. Vakar, & A. Kozulin, Eds., A. Kozulin, Trans.). MIT Press (Original work published 1934).

Wierzbicka, A. (2008). Why there are no 'colour universals' in language and thought. *Journal of the Royal Anthropological Institute, 14*(2), 107–125.

CHAPTER 3

Illusio and Ethos in Academia

Abstract This chapter provides an analysis of the ethos of academics in neoliberal universities with the aim to develop an ethics for academics. More than adding to the large literature dissecting the nefarious impact of neoliberalism, the chapter critiques academics' lack of collective response to the higher education crisis. Framing the discussion around three key factors, which, since the 1980s, have changed the ethos, structures, and roles of universities—namely financialisation, marketisation and managerialism, the chapter uses Bourdieu's concept of illusio to help explain the apparent complicity of academics to reproduce neoliberal practices. Reasons advanced include that of epistemopathy: that knowledge, especially of impending doom, leads to disempowerment. Another key explanation is that neoliberal 'rules of the game' (such as pressure, control, rewards and punishment) only accentuated what was already there: academics' inherent desire for symbolic capital. In fact, the chapter exemplifies complicit behaviours from resignation, radical or critical posturing, increased incivility, to prodigious publication metrics, which show both a loss of meaning and a threat to (or loss of) illusio. The chapter concludes that it is through the difficult and long process of transforming academic habitus that we have any chance of transforming universities.

Keywords Illusio · Ethos · Ethics · Complicity · Habitus · Epistemopathy

L. Monbec and A. Ding, *Recovering Language in Higher Education*, https://doi.org/10.1007/978-3-031-76699-2_3

INTRODUCTION

That universities are in crisis in the UK and many other western countries would seem to be beyond doubt. There is a large body of publication with titles such as 'The Alienated Academic' (Hall, 2018), 'Universities Under Fire' (Jones, 2022), 'Dark Academia: How Universities Die' (Fleming, 2021a), 'Speaking of Universities' (Collini, 2017), 'Dark Academe' (Di Leo, 2024), 'Take Back Higher Education' (Giroux & Giroux, 2004), and 'University Inc: The Corporate Corruption of Higher Education' (Washburn, 2008) and this strand of critique stretches back much earlier too (cf Bill Readings' 1996 publication 'The University in Ruins'). Mirroring existential malaise about universities, and a much broader rise in identity politics, has been the exponential growth of studies on academic identity. Despite some differences and nuances in analyses of the causes of the ongoing crisis affecting universities nearly all evoke 'neoliberalism' as the primary source and sin. The unmasking of neoliberalism 'has become part of political rhetoric, albeit as an almost meaningless insult' (Hartwich, 2009: 4). Boas and Gans-Morse go even further: neoliberalism is a 'conceptual trash heap capable of accommodating multiple distasteful phenomena without much argument as to whether one or the other component really belongs' (2009:156). Busk (2023:2) notes that those in critical or radical fields 'are less likely to take seriously the structures of thought that actually reflect the political forces that govern our lives in concrete ways'. He goes on to claim (idem:4) '[w]e tend to proceed as if our obvious moral superiority relieved us of the responsibility of making an argument'. We duly take note. We accept that the idea and evocation of neoliberalism as it manifests itself in universities is frequently nebulous and acts often as an undefined given of a determining structural force shaping and controlling universities and its agents. It acts as an umbrella term and key word to house a wealth of discontent and critiques of universities.

We will provide a brief summary of *some* of the main features of neoliberalism and its impact on universities and weave this into our analysis of universities and especially of academics. We also need to stress that as disastrous as things are in universities we anticipate that it will get much worse. It seems rebarbative to repeat it here: the impending climate catastrophe; the rise of extreme right-wing/authoritarian governments; rapidly increasing disparities in wealth; the increased likelihood of another, even more deadly, global virus; the annihilation of Palestinians and Russia's war on Ukrainians (being just two of the most visible atrocities being committed) along with the increasing likelihood of other wars, the list could go on much longer. The university risks being a footnote of concerns about the future.

Our main concern in this chapter and the next lies less with repeating the nefarious impact of neoliberalism on universities and more to try to understand the *ethos* of academics in neoliberal universities in order to develop an *ethics* for academics.

We are somewhat reluctant to repeat the litany of ills of neoliberalism because '[n]o matter how much vitriol academics direct at the neoliberal university, none of it seems to make a difference' (Fleming, 2021a:8). Especially, as Davies and Petersen (2005:34) pointedly ask:

> How is it, given that neoliberal discourse can so easily be constituted as monstrous and absurd, that academics appear to have engaged in relatively little systematic or widespread resistance and critique of it?
> Davies and Petersen (2005:34)

Fleming partially responds to this question with:

> More generally, the quietism demonstrated by scholars has been embarrassing. Unlike other high-skilled professions, including medicine and law, academics have generally kowtowed to the steamroller of managerialism. Thomas Docherty (2016, 22) claims that university staff are "among the most conservative, ineffectual and disorganised of workforces" in the post-industrial economy. Some even speak of academic zombies on this score.
> Fleming (2021b:13).

The question, then, is to try to understand why, when there appears to be so much published dissecting and criticising the neoliberal university, 'academics are so bloody supine in the face of so much stuff that is pushed upon them' (a UK professor interviewed by Knights and Clarke (2014:347)), with researchers 'remarkably feeble, almost like marionettes in a puppet show gone awry' (Alvesson et al., 2017:55). After a brief outline of the contours of neoliberal universities, we will turn to Bourdieu to try to understand what Thierry et al., (2023:3) label 'socially organized denial' which appears to characterise academics' collective response to the crisis of neoliberal universities.

Before we move on to the contours of neoliberal universities, a brief word about using Bourdieu as a vehicle for understanding academics. On the face of it, Bourdieu is a poor choice as his 'model of social practice remains fundamentally determinist' (Jenkins, 1989:642). This apparent determinism where the actor 'is no more than a passive reflection of macro-scale social changes being pushed and pulled around as charges particles in a magnetic field' (Faber, 2017:442) is compounded by a hopeless politics:

> What we are left with is a theory of reproduction that displays little faith in subordinate classes and groups and little hope in their ability or willingness to reconstruct the conditions under which they live, work, and learn. Giroux, 1983:274.

Rancière, writing as part of a collective, denounces the uselessness of Bourdieu's politics as '[t]he orphaned fervour of denouncing the system with the disenchanted certitude of its perpetuity' (Collective, 1984:7), with Bourdieu occupying 'the position of eternal denouncer' (Ross, 1991: xii). Not only a determinist and a disenchanted denouncer, we could also add that the attraction to Bourdieu 'resonates with the lived experience of elite academics, offers a form of ersatz radicalism focused on self-transformation, and provides the sociologist with a sense of having an elevated social role' (Riley, 2017:136) as well as being 'hard to imagine a sociological theory whose social ontology is more perfectly aligned with the lifeworld of the chattering classes' (ibid:132).

We have chosen to use Bourdieu, in part, because we hope to demonstrate his concepts, especially *illusio*, help explain the complicity and alignment of academics to reproduce neoliberal practices that accentuate what was already acute among academics, i.e. to exist as an academic is to differ, that is to occupy a distinct, distinctive position. Bourdieu, in an interview with Wacquant, also helps explain the contribution of radical academics to a continuation of injustices:

> The blindness of intellectuals to the social forces which rule the intellectual field, and therefore their practices, is what explains that, collectively, often under very radical airs, the intelligentsia always contribute to the perpetuation of dominant forces
> Wacquant (1989:18).

We will suggest that there are symbolic and cultural capital gains from adopting a 'radical' or 'critical' posture (what might be termed within universities as 'ethical capital') that can be entirely absorbed into universities and commodified both for the benefit of the academic and their university. Being *critical* or *radical* can serve as a.

> terrain for professional and interpersonal status competitions and displays. These latter can be successful in professional terms to the extent that they align correctly with institutional and career imperatives (the article is well placed, the conference paper leads collaboration on a grant application) Whelan, 2015:135.

More colourfully and pointedly, Fleming (once again) laments that academics critical of neoliberal universities would 'still rejoice when their Google Citation Score increases' and, worse, 'would seemingly run over their next of kin in a small jeep if it meant getting published in a "top" journal' (Fleming, 2021a:5).

Neoliberal Universities

Turning now to the contours of neoliberalism, as of 2017, 'neoliberalism' appears in more than 400,000 academic publications (Dunn, 2017:436). Rowlands and Rawolle (2013) reviewed 110 articles in education journals in which neoliberal appeared in the title. Almost half of these articles offered no definition or explanation of neoliberalism, a further quarter provide only a very brief definition or explanation with only the remaining quarter offering substantive definition and explanation. This suggests, at least within the field of education studies (and possibly in other fields), that neoliberalism is a *doxa*. Associated with its status as an *academic doxa* ('neoliberalism' rarely features beyond academic texts and the media preferred by the liberal professional classes) is a host of problems around the definition, scope, coherence, explanatory power and efficacy of neoliberalism to describe, capture and combat global, regional and local economic, political and social capitalist structures and forces at play. This has led many to question or reject neoliberalism as a (politically and theoretically) useful construct. Venugopal (2015: 169) claims that neoliberalism is now shouldering 'an inordinate descriptive and analytical burden in the social sciences'. Dunn (2017) provides an excellent critical overview of the many theoretical failings of neoliberalism as a concept, citing a wide range of highly sceptical positions on the explanatory utility of neoliberalism. Citing Venugopal (2015):

> [t]here is no contemporary body of knowledge that calls itself neoliberalism, no self-described neoliberal theorists that elaborate it, nor policymakers or practitioners that implement it ... Consequently, neoliberalism often features, even in sober academic tracts, in the rhetorical toolkit of caricature and dismissal, rather than analysis and deliberation. Venugopal, 2015:179.

Drawing on Phelan (2014), Weller and O'Neill (2014), and Birch (2015), Springer et al., (2016:11) warn that 'neoliberalism risks ending up as some sort of totalising rhetorical signifier or trope, rather than a concept we can use to reflect the specificity and particularity of human social life'. Despite significant risks of neoliberalism being 'reductive, sacrificing attention to internal complexities and geo-historical specificity' (Hall, 2011:706) and despite our own lack of professional erudition around the complexities of neoliberalism we concur with Hall 'that naming neo-liberalism is politically necessary to give the resistance to its onward march content, focus and a cutting edge' (idem). Otherwise, stuck in *aporia*, we make no headway as we devote our attentions to important but, for our purposes here, esoteric (and largely academic) theoretical discussions beyond the scope of our aims and ambitions here. At the same time, we clearly run the risk of repeating the sins outlined above and risk offering only a faulty, rudimentary and politically sterile account of the ethos of academics in neoliberal universities.

Harvey provides a detailed definition of neoliberalism that we will be guided by:

> Neoliberalism is in the first instance a theory of political economic practices that proposes that human well-being can best be advanced by liberating individual entrepreneurial freedoms and skills within an institutional framework characterized by strong private property rights, free markets and free trade. The role of the state is to create and preserve an institutional framework appropriate to such practices. The state has to guarantee, for example, the quality and integrity of money. It must also set up those military, defence, police and legal structures and functions required to secure private property rights and to guarantee, by force if need be, the proper functioning of markets. Furthermore, if markets do not exist (in areas such as

land, water, education, health care, social security, or environmental pollution) then they must be created, by state action if necessary. But beyond these tasks the state should not venture. State interventions in markets (once created) must be kept to a bare minimum because, according to the theory, the state cannot possibly possess enough information to second-guess market signals (prices) and because powerful interest groups will inevitably distort and bias state interventions (particularly in democracies) for their own benefit.
Harvey, 2007:2.

The salient features of neoliberalism can be distilled from Harvey's rather detailed definition of neoliberalism:

- A focus on individual liberty in the economic sphere
- A strong protection of private property
- Free trade and open markets
- Markets must be created in all or as many areas as possible (including education, health care, transport)
- The state must protect the integrity of markets through the use of force if necessary

Furthermore, neoliberalism is fundamentally a '[a] programme for destroying collective structures which may impede the pure market logic' (Bourdieu, 1998: npng) and, in turn, establishing neoliberalism as a *doxa*, functioning *as if* it were *the* objective truth (Chopra, 2003:421) where a particular point of view, the view of the dominant, 'presents itself as a universal point of view' (Bourdieu, 1998: npng) and thus attempts to contain and foreclose what is thinkable, what is reasonable, what is possible, and what is ethical.

Neoliberal policies within universities, enacted since the 1980s, have changed and are continuing to change the ethos, structures and roles of universities: financialisation, marketisation and managerialism. The accentuated economic role entailed universities embracing applied subjects, vocationalism, productivity and accountability to external stakeholders (especially businesses).

A useful definition of financialisation is provided by Epstein (2005:3) as: 'the increasing role of financial motives, financial markets, financial actors and financial institutions in the operation of the domestic and international economies'. The main commodity universities financialise is knowledge. One of the most significant ways in which knowledge has been commodified and financialised is charging and/or increasing student fees (especially for international students) and relegating students to consumers and clients of educational services and products. Underpinning charging or increasing fees (often very substantially) is the premise that paying for their education (and in the process accumulating huge often life-time debts) ensures students invest (in both senses of the term) in their education, forces them to make rational career and educational choices and promises that they can be competitive in volatile global job markets. Not only is knowledge financialised through students buying an education. Universities also invest heavily in commercialising research, setting up their own companies and contracting expertise to large companies (including pharmaceutical companies).

New Public Management (NPM) has exercised considerable influence in universities where each department or school (and one could add each and every academic) is a self-funding cost centre and changes to the school/department can only be taken if they align with the corporate vision and financial objectives of the university. This has resulted in hierarchies of disciplines where profitable centres such as business schools, law schools and those that attract external research funding that provide tangible or perceived benefits and profits to the university to large organisations (such as the military or governments) or companies are much more powerful than those disciplines that offer more intangible benefits and little or no profit. The closure of language programmes and whole departments now regularly features in higher education news (e.g. University of Kent, University of Aberdeen, University of Hull). Usually, a well written indignant petition ensues, signed by many luminary academics, a number of passionate and indignant letters are published, campaigns are launched showing the economic benefits of studying languages, the relevant VC or senior academic expresses his or her regret, but closure is usually the outcome as languages do not generate (enough) profit. If a discipline does not have a (buoyant) external market it risks extinction. The UK is currently witnessing widespread redundancies (estimated at well over 2000 in July 2024) across a very large number of universities (60 and rising weekly), including the University of Hull where one in six academics are to be made redundant, and where, across the sector, languages, arts and humanities are particularly hard hit.

Marketisation is central to the neoliberal project and to the neoliberal university:

Markets are driven by consumer choice, and choice means competition between providers. Competition means that the supply side [the universities as providers] must continuously seek to gain advantage in the market in terms of price, quality of service or the development of innovative products or services. This will serve to stimulate innovation and promote efficiency and lower costs.
Fosket, 2011:29.

Marketisation calculates that students operate rationally (in a highly reductive sense of students striving for the maximum return on their investment in education) and will necessarily strive and compete to enter the 'best' universities, on the 'best' courses. Consequently, universities will have to raise their standards in order to attract the 'best' students. Competition in the higher education market, so the argument goes, will result in standards being driven up across the sector. To assist students in making an economically rational choice of course and university there are now a number of ranking organisations that provide information for students, academics, governments and other bodies which claim to objectively rank universities in many facets. Rankings serve as a proxy for quality and distinction. The methodologies for ranking are highly contested and the politest way of putting it is that there is a lack of scientific rigour. Financialisation, as we saw, produces hierarchies among disciplines within a university and across universities, but marketisation and rankings produce hierarchies among universities, regionally, nationally and globally. Through stratification of universities, we now have first-, second- and third-class universities.

One remarkable consequence of marketisation is a narrowing of the diversity of knowledge and universities. Competition was and is supposed to encourage distinction between universities, each with a singular identity to allow diversity and distinction within the global education market, yet the discourses, subjects, research and visions of universities end up looking remarkably similar. A flattening of diversity, a uniformity of courses on offer, similar promises of developing soft skills and employability, similar promises of an enriching student experience and the same visions to tackle global challenges and crises are all presented in university marketing as unique to their university. Competition and marketisation have been extremely effective in rendering universities unable and possibly unwilling to be distinctive. All universities are subject to the same very limited options in that they are all subject to coercive control; rankings and performance indicators and chasing the same income streams. Universities are trapped within a highly constrained marketised logic.

In order to effectively implement the processes and policies associated with financialisation and marketisation of universities, managerialism has been incorporated from the business world. Managerialism refers to corporate systems of organisation and especially control and discipline. Managerialism encompasses 'discourses and practices established in the private market such as corporate modes of speech, professional administrators, line management, and competition for resources' (Hyde et al., 2013: 42). Consequently, academics' research and teaching interests are subordinate and organisational objectives are primary and conveyed and impressed through 'mission' statements, 'goals', research polices, development plans and university strategy plans. These objectives are structured and enforced through systems of monitoring and surveillance where academics are subjected to performance objectives (such as obtaining grants, publishing, obtaining scores on student evaluations) and ongoing individual professional development reviews. Traditional academic self-regulation and democratic control, vague and largely collegial as it was, has been replaced with managerial means of control, rewards (and punishment), monitoring and remedial training. Olssen (2001:45) captures, very succinctly, some of the major contours of neoliberal management in universities:

Mode of control	'Hard' Managerialism; contractual specification between principal-agent; autocratic control
Management function	Managers; line-management; cost-centres
Goals	Maximise outputs; financial profit; efficiency; massification; privatisation
Work relations	Competitive; hierarchical; workload indexed to market; corporate loyalty; no adverse criticism of university
Accountability	Audit; monitoring; consumer-managerial; performance indicators; output-based *(ex-post)*
Marketing	Centres of excellence; competition; corporate image; branding; public relations
Pedagogy/teaching	Semesterisation; slenderisation of courses; modularisation; distance learning; summer schools; vocational mode 2 learning
Research	Externally funded; contestable; separated from teaching; controlled by government or external agency

ACADEMIC ETHOS

You will note that the above from Olssen (2001) dates to over 20 years ago and attentive readers will also have noted that many of the sources cited above also date by 10–15 years. This is expressly to demonstrate just how long these policies and practices have been in place and how little has changed and what has changed is only an acceleration and deterioration of what was noted 20 plus years ago. It also brings us back to the central concern of this chapter: the ethos of academics in universities. More specifically, despite apparent widespread knowledge among academics of the many failings of neoliberal universities along with frequent published denunciations of neoliberal universities, why are academics *so bloody supine?* If academics appears to suffer 'anomie and alienation' (Beck & Young, 2005:185) and *if* academics are 'transparent but empty, unrecognisable to ourselves' (Ball, 2016:1054), *why* have some academics 'enthusiastically embraced the new managerial opportunities that have been opened up and have indeed pushed through the very restructuring that others so bitterly resent' (Beck & Young, 2005:194)? Is it reasonable or fair or serve any purpose to castigate academics when the structural forces that shape their professional lives in so many facets appear so complete and so suffocating?

One thread of an answer to these questions relies on an argument that aspects of neoliberal policies in higher education, particularly metrics, competition, hierarchies, distinctions and rewards, *accentuate*, albeit in a highly distorted fashion and stripped of any real or imagined past ethos, what was already part of the *habitus* of academics, the *doxa* of academic fields and the *capitals* at stake and struggled over within all academic fields. Consequently, neoliberal policies met with only feeble collective opposition. A *second* thread of an answer to these questions is connected to the first but focuses more on what (Connor, 2021) labels epistemopathy, which is 'the pathos of knowledge, that is, the inner as subjective life of knowing' (Connor, 2021:13). *Knowing* that the university is rife with injustices and knowing that 'complaints and criticisms will not lead to substantive change ... we fear they only lead to cynicism and defeatism and become excuses for academic narcissism and careerism' (Alvesson et al., 2017:138). Knowledge is, in this case, disempowerment. Academic utopias and manifestos can also offer a cruel optimism where the perceived implausibility of radical change is not only shared by the sceptical reader but also, one suspects, by the authors themselves who nonetheless benefit as a 'radical' through a nihilism where their values cannot find the world in a world without values.

The linchpin of the explanation for an accentuation of what was already part of the *habitus* of academics—that neoliberal policies continue to exploit—lies in Bourdieu's concept of illusio and, more specifically, how illusio is related to *ethos* as/of academic practice.

> [A]gents are drawn to a field because of the field illusio that presupposes and promises an ethos, values and normative orientation. Fields are laden with ethical doxas and illusio that promise rewards and recognition and fulfilling aspirations but also they are arenas for (widespread) 'blighted hope' or 'frustrated promise'.
> Bourdieu, 1984: 150

The illusio of academic fields have a strong ethos, requiring an investment in the game: 'the mere fact of playing, and not by way of a "contract", that the game is worth playing, that it is "worth the candle", and this collusion is the very basis of their competition' (Bourdieu & Wacquant, 1992:98). Ethics and normative values are doubly inscribed in the history of academic fields and in the habitus of agents through:

- Professional associations (conferences, awards, prizes and rewards, scholarly journals, codes of professional ethics);
- An academic organisational unit (hiring, probation and promotion of staff);
- Publishers;
- Styles of subjectivity/judgement (criteria for assessing the value of work, concept of rigour, practices that identify agents as a member of the disciplinary community);
- Narrative(s) of the discipline's development and legitimacy;
- A body of accumulated knowledge and skills;
- A (global) discursive community with a common language.

(adapted from D'Agostino, 2012).

What appears to be essential to the illusio of academic fields is autonomy: 'an exceptional measure of collective collegiate autonomy over their conditions of professional training, certification of professional competence, and conditions of work and practice' (Beck & Young,

2005:185) or 'this demand for autonomy is expressed through the assertion of the right of scientists to settle scientific questions ("mathematics for mathematicians"), in the name of the specific legitimacy that is conferred upon them by their competence' (Bourdieu, 1991:17).

Illusio especially through collusio provides a shared sense of purpose and competition (Bourdieu, 2000:145) and within academic fields competition plays out for various forms of field-dependent capitals (cultural, social and economic) which, when configured in field-specific ways, leads to symbolic capital. Symbolic capital takes the form of prestige, esteem, legitimation, recognition and distinction, and those with significant symbolic capital have a 'socially recognized authority to act' (Swartz, 2013: 102) upon agents in the field.

> Symbolic capital enables forms of domination which imply dependence on those who can be dominated by it, since it only exists through the esteem, recognition, belief, credit, confidence of others, and can only be perpetuated so long as it succeeds in obtaining belief in its existence.
> Bourdieu, 2000: 166.

Ethos and ethics saturate Bourdieu's description of symbolic capital. Values, normative distinctions, and strong evaluations enables a hierarchy of agents within fields. Academics are especially prone to struggling over individual distinction because 'to exist as an academic is to differ, that is to occupy a distinct, distinctive position' (Bourdieu, 1983:338). Those that are dominated within an academic field, those lacking in the most powerful configurations of capital which foreclose symbolic capital, are 'not acknowledged as worthy in a given field or culture' (Pellandini-Simányi, 2014:668). The sacred 'has its profane complement, all distinction generates its own vulgarity' (Bourdieu, 1990:196). The pharmakonic and paradoxical essence of symbolic capital lies in an 'egotistical quest for satisfaction of *amour propre* which is, at the same time, a fascinated pursuit of the approval of others' (Bourdieu, 2000:166). Symbolic capital 'rescues agents from insignificance, the absence of importance and of meaning' (ibid: 242). However:

> We must, indeed, resign ourselves to admitting that, short of demanding of everyone at every moment the extraordinary dispositions of the saint, the genius, or the hero, one can obtain ordinary reason or virtue only from a

social order capable of making these into a specific form of well-understood self-interest
Bourdieu, 1991:22

This Machiavellian republic 'in which citizens are virtuous because they have a vested interest in virtue' (idem), is instigated through illuso—the allure and rules of the game—and habitus. Habitus can be understood as 'a principle of repetition and conservation' (Bourdieu, 2000:159) because 'the responses habitus generates without calculation appear as adapted, coherent and immediately intelligible' within a field. Habitus promises a 'feel for the game', a generative principle where when/if habitus and field align, practitioners achieve subjective expectations of objective probabilities, and where academics can exercise practical mastery in their field. Habitus entails dispositions, including ones pertaining to ethos, inculcated by objective conditions and these spur 'aspirations and practices objectively compatible with these objective requirements, the most improbable practices are excluded, as *unthinkable*, or... inclines agents to make a virtue of necessity ... to refuse what is anyway refused and to love the inevitable' (Bourdieu, 1977:77). Objective regularities determine what constitutes reasonable and unreasonable actions and conduct (idem). What is reasonable or unreasonable, thinkable and unthinkable, probable or unlikely, is also related to what is desirable and worthy—of ethos and ethics.

Lost Illusio

The brief outline above of observations by Bourdieu offers a means to understand academics in neoliberal universities especially, but not only, in terms of a lack of resistance to neoliberal policies. Through incentives and pressures, accentuating the already inherent desire for symbolic capital, neoliberal policies distort, mangle and corrupt illusio. The game worth playing—apparently the only game—is one that empties academic life of meaning. What is under threat—or already lost depending on your point of view—is the illusio of academic fields, what makes the game worth playing, what gives academic life meaning.

There are 6 million academics, working in 17,000 universities producing 1.5 million articles a year as of 2009 (Hyland, 2016). According to Alevesson, Gabriel and Paulesen (2017:7), 50% of published articles in the social sciences remain uncited within two years of publication and 32% remain uncited after five years. Haufe (2023:229) suggests pretty much the same. In the humanities, however, less than 10% of articles have at least one citation after two years and less than 18% after five. And Haufe draws the conclusion that humanities scholars 'can reasonably expect to have their research used by no one' (ibid:230). One significance of this is that, as noted by Bourdieu (1988), citations are a proxy for symbolic capital, and, as such, in the struggle for symbolic capital in neoliberal universities, there will be many many more losers than winners both within disciplines and across disciplines, compounded too by important differences in journal rejection rates between academics working in high and low income countries (Patel & Kim, 2007), and further compounded by a lack of linguistic capital for academics working in languages other than English which has a hegemonic grip on almost if not all disciplines.

Bibliometrics are incorporated into the habitus of academics as they are used to distinguish academics through classifying, recruiting and promoting which ensures ferocious competition between academics. This (summarised from Macfarlane, 2021) often leads to dubious and unethical practices such as including excessive self-citation and citing papers from the journal they wish to publish in to curry favour. Even something as doxic as co-authoring is subject to symbolic power where hierarchical power (a PhD supervisor, a senior colleague for example) can impose (often with complicity) co-authorship on dominated colleagues and students while having contributed little to no writing nor intellectual participation. Co-authorship is rising, however, 48% of 13,000 articles analysed did not meet the Vancouver protocol and international standard for joint authorship (Sauermann and Haessier, 2017, cited in Macfarlane, 2021).

Along with publishing prodigiously and in prestigious journals and supervising PhD, generation of grant income forms the core of academic survival and as a platform for prestige (failure to meet these three criteria can lead to relegation to 'teaching-only' status). Applying for prestigious grants takes considerable resources, time and effort (with high chances of rejection), encourages conservative research and promotes 'cronyism' (Macfarlane, 2021) with funds concentrated around elite institutions and powerful academics.

There are other means of struggling over symbolic capitals and other capitals beyond citation as a proxy for esteem. Bourdieu (1991) discusses delegated capital, that is the transfer of capital from an institution to an academic or group. If an institution is dominant in the hierarchy of universities (usually measured by dubious metrics) and has 'elite' status, this will be conferred on or delegated to academics working there. Furthermore, and conforming with the rules of neoliberal academia, to obtain symbolic capital, digital self-promotion/exploitation is expected and normalised, where successes (however trivial), publications, plenaries, grants, promotions, are all very publicly celebrated and shared while those—especially women—who are reticent and uncomfortable with entrepreneurial self-promotion are marginalised and remain less visible in the marketplace for attention/distinction (Aslan & Jaworska, 2024).

Faced with an endless struggle over symbolic capital, with, at best, fragile and temporary successes, except for the very few, academics seem consigned to 'make a virtue of necessity' (Bourdieu, 1977: 77). Bourdieu (2000) provides a useful insight into why, despite a manifest distortion of academic ethos, those that are dominated within universities persist nonetheless to play the game:

> [E]ven the harshest established order provides some advantages of order that are not lightly sacrificed, indignation, revolt and transgressions (in starting a strike for example) are always difficult and painful and almost always costly, both materially and psychologically.
> Bourdieu, 2000:231.

What remains, within neoliberal academia, is the *illusio*. In their study of early career researchers (ECRs), Stratford, Watson and Paull (2024) found that despite world-weariness and considering universities 'brutal', ECRs wanted to combat neoliberalism in universities, wanted their work to be relevant and meaningful, be autonomous, exercise intellectual freedom, with the dominant desire:

> related to higher education's transformational potential and intrinsic worth: being driven by discovery and the quest for new knowledge, including in terms of innovation; being intellectually challenged and stimulating intellectual discussion; problem solving in a particular field; being passionate about interdisciplinary and transdisciplinary research; and sharing all that with students, peers, and members of society.
> Stratford, Watson and Paull, 2024:269.

However, the trope of disillusioned and distressed academics persists and in Kalfa, Wilkinson and Gollan's (2018) case study they found academics were compliant and complicit with neoliberal policy changes, focusing on increasing their own capital(s), where vocal and visible resistance was sparse, and those challenges made by academics were only when their own careers were jeopardised in some way (promotion for example). Resistance took the form of silence, neglect or exit. Respondents' behaviour, according to the authors, 'accentuated what they had decried' (idem:286), e.g. the collapse of collegiality. In slightly different ways both Reay (2004) and Schmidt (2000) emphasise that while professional classes and academics are liberal on distant social issues, they are neglectful and perhaps intolerant of confronting the politics and ethics of their own practices and fields. This tendency may accentuate as the academic habitus of more recent academics, those that have only known and experienced neoliberal higher education, becomes founded on more instrumental ambitions and expectations (Beck & Young, 2005:194). This, aligned with increasing bullying and mobbing in higher education, signals a prevalent and increasing lack of civility in universities (Prevost & Hunt, 2018). This tendency to a lack of civility might be connected with academics who develop '[a] hyper-sensitivity about status, identity and self-esteem [that] make narcissism rampant' (Alvesson et al., 2017:71). Or, as prosaically put by Billig (2013:155), becoming 'a knob head'.

Non-alignment with institutional goals can render academics a '"moral hazard," to which increased discipline, managerial control and technologies of intimidation are the rational response' (Webb, 2018:97 cited in Fleming, 2021a). Critiquing neoliberal universities *in general* is a very safe and profitable practice as both academics and universities can benefit from this critique through accruing symbolic capital measured by metrics of citations, esteem and recognition. Indeed, as noted by Alvesson et al., (2017:65), critical academics who enjoy a middle-class lifestyle are content to criticise power and institutional obstacles thereby enhancing their radical credentials (while refusing to help institutions to transform) and profiting while complaining (idem:53). What *is* a moral hazard for universities is when this critique turns to specific named institutions and agents thereby risking damaging their brand and reputation.

A profound loss of meaning, within some disciplines, can also be detected. Sociology and, more broadly, social theory and the social sciences, provide prime examples. Alvesson et al. (2017) offer a trenchant but useful starting point to contemplate this loss of meaning.

Social science is undermined by playing the publishing game of rankings and citations to increase academics' and institutional prestige rendering publications meaningless and valueless with no wider social uses. Minor and trivial additions to literature are frequent and, at best, only meaningful to a minute sub-field of a discipline. Disciplines, fragmented into small sub-fields with their own jargons, conventions and rituals, represent highly parochial interests and concerns (idem:7): 'an ingrown sectarianism' (Burawoy, 2005:17). No significant effort or desire is demonstrated to share with audiences beyond academia (not even with those in their broader discipline). Both Thorpe (2022) and Shapin (2005) (among numerous commentaries) note that a lack of a broader readership for social theory/sociology (and philosophy)—'readership drops off like a cliff face' (Shapin, 2005:239)—should be a serious moral concern for academics working in these fields, especially, as Thorpe warns, 'the hypertrophy of narrowly technical reason accompanies the atrophy of reason in public' (idem:150).

Hyper-specialisation in sociology (and other disciplines), or disciplinary fractal processes (Abbott, 2010), result in not only a highly specific technical language and policing of these sub-field boundaries, but academics within these sub-fields experience their own academic identities not through a general disciplinary concern with a broad and general understanding of social forces and society but through their relatively smaller and disconnected concerns. One consequence of which is that in a discipline like sociology (or a field like applied linguistics) 'radical' or 'critical' forms can and do co-exist with hyper-conventional forms as 'cognitive territory is willingly and disdainfully abandoned and ceded by sociology's professional exclusions' (Thorpe, 2022:224). This fractalisation or fragmentation of disciplines with parochial concerns and interests means, as we have seen, that claiming a contribution to a sub-field 'usually amounts to trivial additions to small outposts of literature only meaningful to tiny research microtribes' (Alvesson et al., 2017:7). Furthermore, Campbell (2019) laments that so little progress has been made in sociology in terms of the core theoretical concerns of sociology (the relationship between structure and agency for example) not because 'sociologists have tried and failed but rather because so few have even tried' (idem:110), focused as they are on their sub-fields and micro-tribes.

Campbell (and others as we shall see) provide a different sort of critique of sociology than the one that sociology lacks a critical orientation. In fact, their critique points in the opposite direction. For Campbell, a fundamental problem with sociology is that it has been:

> ... repeatedly hijacked to act as a vehicle, either for advancing an ideology, or indulging in moralism, thereby diverting resources away from the primary task of advancing the understanding of social life
> Campbell, 2019:84.

Baehr (2019), in a complementary vein to Campbell, analyses the motivations and effects of unmasking in social theory. Unmasking elevates and provides distinction—above and beyond the uninitiated—to those operating with social theory (idem:130) and is 'heavily freighted with moral earnestness and political intent' (idem:1):

> ... the new spectatorial Left has an essentially Gothic view of society. It sees power everywhere, suffusing all spaces, bodies as well as minds, a preternatural force that can never be defeated, only endlessly "interrogated". Confronting power does not mean addressing harmful practices, putting forward concrete alternatives and mobilizing support for them. Confronting power means critique, a thorough unmasking of the system... The cultural Left's disdainful tone and rebarbative language is not a policy. It is an open invitation for other political forces to move into abandoned territory.
> Idem:134.

Stypinska (2020:4) characterises the critical-academic as a 'theory-clown with bloody tears'. She captures the current paradoxical and debilitating forms of critique 'wherein an excess of criticism coincides with a steadfast conviction in both the lack of alternatives to the existing socioeconomic order and the impossibility of its qualitative change' (ibid:8), and concomitantly the critical-academic constantly and assiduously avoids any irreversible political commitments and gestures.

More broadly, in the humanities and social sciences, Campbell (2019) lambasts the belief that 're-dressing grievances justifies rejecting the very idea of impartial scientific inquiry' (idem:86). In addition, he argues that 'turns' in sociology (e.g. digital, relational, critical, cultural, historic, activist, linguistic, practice, spatial, peripheral, mobility, ...), and we could say the same about applied linguistics, *might* represent progress but it is also a turning away, a turning one's back on something (idem:95), a form of negligence, loss and forgetting. For the ambitious academic, a 'turn' represents career opportunities. All sorts of rewards, recognition and accolades are available for distinction, novelty and originality (idem:18). However, as noted by Abbott (2006:58), turns can result in amnesia, and the new wheel can look very much the same as the old wheel.

Academic life and practices within neoliberal regimes, as discussed in this chapter, could be pithily summarised as follows:

> It may have no meaning and be painful but everything about it makes sense – the successes, the failures, even the (perceived) injustices and disappointments.
> Alvesson et al., 2017:33.

CONCLUSION

What is striking throughout this chapter is the epistemopathic traces and tropes of *knowing* within neoliberal universities. This chapter is littered with *pathos*, a stubborn commitment to an (academic) *illusio*, combined with a sense of loss, a sense of futility and meaninglessness. Nonetheless, through the practices of either active or passive complicity (naively or cynically) or of ineffectual resistance (from resignation to expressing utopian desires), academics still participate in the struggles for legitimisation and symbolic capital. Historical, inherent and integral in academic fields, but, within neoliberal regimes, struggles for symbolic capital take on a new intensity, distorting and corrupting *ethos*. Universities are rife with anxiety, stress, paranoia, bullying and harassment, disillusionment, disengagement, alienation, anomie, control and discipline, alongside self-aggrandisement, self-promotion, the relentless pursuit of distinction, rewards, promotion and recognition (however trivial and ephemeral), and persistent exaggerations of (self) importance and impact. Yet, we also *know* despite all this, triggering *pathos*, inspiring colleagues, embodying an academic *ethos*, who continue to struggle to enact and embody values and principles very much at odds with neoliberal ones.

The sense of loss of meaning in academia is doubly profound, not only in terms of habitus and ethos, but also in terms of the fragmentation and loss of meaning within/of/for disciplines. The purpose of social theory and sociology (which surely must form the bedrock of any understanding and critique of universities) is contested, with very different views on the roles, purposes and consequences of *critique*. And, indeed, who benefits from operating as a 'radical' within these fields. A debilitating sense of collective disciplinary disempowerment to understand *and* transform practices permeates this chapter.

Knowing that neoliberal universities corrupt academic *ethos* is not enough to change much. It is a 'scholastic illusion' (Bourdieu, 2000:172), whereby:

> [P]eople describe resistance to domination in the language of consciousness ... ignoring the extraordinary inertia which results from the inscription of social structures in bodies, for lack of a dispositional theory of practices. While making things explicit can help, only a thoroughgoing process of counter training involving repeated exercises, can, like an athlete's training, durably transform habitus.
> Idem

This gives us a measure of what needs to be done: raising consciousness is useful but it is through the much more difficult and much longer process of transforming academic habitus that we have any chance of transforming universities. Habitus entails ethos and through ethos we can arrive at an *ethics*. This will be the focus of the next chapter, within the fields of language education and, more specifically, English for Academic Purposes.

Coda.

In this brief coda, we want to change register and offer something more personal in terms of our own perspectives and experiences of working in universities. We want to do this in part because we operate very clearly in a highly dominated field, in many ways an atypical field within universities, and our habitus, our ethos, has been shaped by this experience. It has afforded us a particular vantage point on universities and a keen motivation to want to contribute to ethics within universities and within language education more narrowly.

Our professional experiences, teaching—TESOL, EAP, ESP, rhetoric, semiotics, and teacher education and development—in universities, totals more than 50 years in four countries (France, the UK, Hong Kong and Singapore). We both currently work at the University of Leeds as practitioners of EAP where our daily professional lives are entangled in complex relationships with academics, colleagues, students and professional staff, associations and professional bodies. At a deeply *untheoretical* level we have had, throughout our professional careers (and we imagine that many of you have witnessed or experienced this), visceral experiences of, for example, incivility, prejudices of all sorts, severe ethical dissonance, harmful gossiping, careerism, hypocrisy, bullying, nepotism, managerialism, academic snobbery, narcissism, and physical and verbal aggression. Our own everyday entanglements with others has not led to a simple condemnation of others, tempting as it is, but of uncomfortable reflections on our contributions to academia and colleagues' lives.

We work on teaching and scholarship contracts, and like many universities in the UK, teaching and scholarship of teaching and learning (SoTL) are being given more prominence, incentives and rewards because of the importance of metrics and rankings of teaching to recruit and satisfy students. The rewards and distinctions for teaching have led to, in our view, the same logics of distortion of ethos as for research. Many more teaching focused academics are now promoted to professor for contributions to leadership and student education (not necessarily through any significant external contributions such as pedagogical research publications), an increase in scholarship of teaching and learning (through sponsored projects and publications) and there is a proliferation of Oscar type ceremonies celebrating and rewarding teaching with certificates and photos. There are many more senior teaching roles and titles proliferate at all levels (there appears to be more levels of hierarchy in academia than the military). There is a proliferation of projects, for illustrative purposes, to improve EDI, belonging, well-being, pedagogies of care, decolonisation, uses of AI, feedback and access to higher education. We do not wish to focus on these initiatives, even though some raise serious ethical and political concerns, but simply note that in the struggles for distinction and symbolic capital academics are as likely to manipulate chances of personal success in the teaching domain as in the research domain. We have witnessed gross exaggeration of teaching impact, contradictions between the profession of social justice and professional behaviour, appropriation of a collective effort for personal gain, a lack of desire to teach but a strong desire to direct teaching and so on.

Our everyday professional lives, while having important moments of joy and hope, also contain potentially debilitating experiences that are corrosive and could all too easily lead to cynicism and resignation. Not only that, but perhaps worse, we did not want to slip into an unreflexive stupor which exonerated our own actions: to exempt ourselves from some critical scrutiny.

This is why we wrote this chapter, to give us a theoretical lens to understand and explain what is felt and observed every day and more importantly, as we will attempt in Chapter 5 *Heresy, Ethics and Scholarship*, to outline an ethics of being in academia. One that goes beyond a pathos to an ethos.

REFERENCES

Abbott, A. (2006). Reconceptualizing knowledge accumulation in sociology. *The American Sociologist, 37*(2), 57–66.

Abbott, A. (2010). *Chaos of disciplines*. University of Chicago Press

Alvesson, M., Gabriel, Y., & Paulsen, R. (2017). *Return to meaning: A social science with something to say*. Oxford University Press.

Aslan, E., & Jaworska, S. (2024). Standing 'in' and 'out' from the crowd in a small genre: Proximity and positioning in applied linguists' email signatures. *Applied Linguistics, amae019.*

Baehr, P. (2019). *The unmasking style in social theory*. Routledge.

Ball, S. J. (2016). Subjectivity as a site of struggle: Refusing neoliberalism? *British Journal of Sociology of Education, 37*(8), 1129–1146.

Beck, J., & Young, M. F. (2005). The assault on the professions and the restructuring of academic and professional identities: A Bernsteinian analysis. *British Journal of Sociology of Education, 26*(2), 183–197.

Billig, M. (2013). *Learn to write badly: How to succeed in the social sciences*. Cambridge.

Birch, K. (2015). *We have never been neoliberal*. Zero Books.

Boas, T. C., & Gans-Morse, J. (2009). Neoliberalism: From new liberal philosophy to anti-liberal slogan. *Studies in Comparative International Development, 44*(2), 137–161.

Bourdieu, P. (1977). *Outline of a theory of practice*. Cambridge University Press.

Bourdieu, P. (1983). The field of cultural production, or: The economic world reversed. *Poetics, 12*(4–5), 311–356.

Bourdieu, P. (1984). *Distinction: A social critique of the judgement of taste*. Routledge.

Bourdieu, P. (1988). *Homo academicus*. Stanford University Press.

Bourdieu, P. (1990). *In other words: Essays toward a reflexive sociology*. Stanford University Press.

Bourdieu, P. (1991). The peculiar history of scientific reason. *Sociological Forum, 6*(3), 3–26.

Bourdieu, P. (1998). The essence of neoliberalism. *Le Monde Diplomatique. English Edition*, 12.

Bourdieu, P. (2000). *Pascalian meditations*. Stanford University Press.

Bourdieu, P., & Wacquant, L. J. (1992). *An invitation to reflexive sociology*. University of Chicago Press.

Burawoy, M. (2005). 2004 American Sociological Association presidential address: For public sociology. *The British Journal of Sociology, 56*(2), 259–294.

Busk, L. (2023). *Democracy in spite of the demos: From Arendt to the Frankfurt School*. Rowman & Littlefield.

Campbell, C. (2019). *Has sociology progressed?* Springer.

Chopra, R. (2003). Neoliberalism as doxa: Bourdieu's theory of the state and the contemporary Indian discourse on globalization and liberalization. *Cultural Studies, 17*(3–4), 419–444.

Collective. (1984). 'L'empire du sociologue'. *Révoltes Logiques, 7.*

Collini, S. (2017). *Speaking of universities*. Verso Books.

Connor, S. (2021). *The madness of knowledge: On wisdom, ignorance and fantasies of knowing*. Reaktion Books.

D'Agostino, F. (2012). Disciplinarity and the growth of knowledge. *Social Epistemology, 26*(3–4), 331–350.

Davies, B., & Petersen, E. B. (2005). Intellectual workers (un) doing neoliberal discourse. *International Journal of Critical Psychology, 13*(1), 32–54.

Di Leo, J. R. (2024). *Dark academe: Capitalism, theory, and the death drive in higher education*. Springer Nature.

Docherty, T. (2016). *Complicity: Criticism between collaboration and commitment*. Rowman & Littlefield.

Dunn, B. (2017). Against neoliberalism as a concept. *Capital & Class, 41*(3), 435–454.

Epstein, G. A. (Ed.). (2005). *Financialization and the world economy*. Edward Elgar Publishing.

Faber, A. (2017). From false premises to false conclusions: On Pierre Bourdieu's alleged sociological determinism. *The American Sociologist, 48*, 436–452.

Fleming, P. (2021a). *Dark academia: How universities die*. Pluto Press.

Fleming, P. (2021b). The ghost university: Academe from the ruins. *Emancipations: A Journal of Critical Social Analysis, 1*(1), Article 4.

Fosket, N. (2011). Markets, government, funding and the marketisation of UK higher education. In M. Molesworth, R. Scullion, & E. Nixon (Eds.), *The marketisation of higher education and the student as consumer* (pp. 39–52). Routledge.

Giroux, H. A. (1983). Theories of reproduction and resistance in the new sociology of education: A critical analysis. *Harvard Educational Review, 53*(3), 257–293.

Giroux, H. A., & Giroux, S. S. (2004). *Take back higher education: Race, youth, and the crisis of democracy in the post-civil rights era.* Macmillan.

Hall, R. (2018). *The alienated academic: The struggle for autonomy inside the university.* Springer.

Hall, S. (2011). The neo-liberal revolution. *Cultural Studies, 25*(6), 705–728.

Hartwich, O. M. (2009). *Neoliberalism: The genesis of a political swear-word.* https://oliverhartwich.com/wp-content/uploads/2015/02/neolibera lism.pdf

Harvey, D. (2007). *A brief history of neoliberalism.* Oxford University Press.

Haufe, C. (2023). *Do the humanities create knowledge?* Cambridge University Press.

Hyde, A., Clarke, M., & Drennan, J. (2013). The changing role of academics and the rise of managerialism. In B. Molesworth, R. Scullion, & E. Nixon (Eds.), *The academic profession in Europe: New tasks and new challenges* (pp. 39–52). Springer.

Hyland, K. (2016). Academic publishing and the myth of linguistic injustice. *Journal of Second Language Writing, 31,* 58–69.

Jenkins, R. (1989). Language, symbolic power and communication: Bourdieu's Homo Academicus. *Sociology, 23*(4), 639–645.

Jones, S. (2022). *Universities under fire.* Springer International Publishing.

Kalfa, S., Wilkinson, A., & Gollan, P. J. (2018). The academic game: Compliance and resistance in universities. *Work, Employment and Society, 32*(2), 274–291.

Kolsaker, A. (2008). Academic professionalism in the managerialist era: A study of English universities. *Studies in Higher Education, 33*(5), 513–525.

Knights, D., & Clarke, C. A. (2014). It's a bittersweet symphony, this life: Fragile academic selves and insecure identities at work. *Organization Studies, 35*(3), 335–357.

Macfarlane, B. (2021). The neoliberal academic: Illustrating shifting academic norms in an age of hyper-performativity. *Educational Philosophy and Theory, 53*(5), 459–468.

Olssen, M. (2001). *The neo-liberal appropriation of tertiary education policy: Accountability, research and academic freedom.* New Zealand Association for Research in Education.

Patel, V., & Kim, Y. R. (2007). Contribution of low-and middle-income countries to research published in leading general psychiatry journals, 2002–2004. *The British Journal of Psychiatry, 190*(1), 77–78.

Pellandini-Simányi, L. (2014). Bourdieu, ethics and symbolic power. *The Sociological Review, 62*(4), 651–674.

Phelan, S. (2014). Critiquing neoliberalism: Three interrogations and a defense. In L. A. Lievrouw (Ed.), *Challenging communication research* (pp. 27–41). Peter Lang.

Prevost, C., & Hunt, E. (2018). Bullying and mobbing in academe: A literature. *European Scientific Journal, 14*(8), 15.

Readings, B. (1996). *The university in ruins.* Harvard University Press.

Reay, D. (2004). Cultural capitalists and academic habitus: Classed and gendered labour in UK higher education. *Women's Studies International Forum, 27*(1), 31–39.

Riley, D. (2017). Bourdieu's class theory: The academic as revolutionary. *Catalyst: A Journal of Theory & Strategy, 1*(2), 107–136.

Ross, K. (1991). Translator's introduction. In J. Rancière (Ed.), *The ignorant schoolmaster: Five lessons in intellectual emancipation* (pp. vii–xxiii). Stanford University Press.

Rowlands, J., & Rawolle, S. (2013). Neoliberalism is not a theory of everything: A Bourdieuian analysis of illusio in educational research. *Critical Studies in Education, 54*(3), 260–272.

Sauermann, H., & Haeussler, C. (2017). Authorship and contribution disclosures. *Science Advances, 3*(11), e1700404.

Schmidt, J. (2000). *Disciplined minds: A critical look at salaried professionals and the soul-battering system that shapes their lives.* Rowman & Littlefield.

Springer, S., Birch, K., & MacLeavy, J. (Eds.). (2016). *The handbook of neoliberalism* (Vol. 12). Routledge.

Shapin, S. (2005). Hyperprofessionalism and the crisis of readership in the history of science. *Isis, 96*(2), 238–243.

Stratford, E., Watson, P., & Paull, B. (2024). What impedes and enables flourishing among early career academics? *Higher Education, 88*(1), 259–277.

Stypinska, D. (2020). *On the genealogy of critique: Or how we have become decadently indignant.* Routledge.

Swartz, D. L. (2013). *Symbolic power, politics, and intellectuals: The political sociology of Pierre Bourdieu.* University of Chicago Press.

Thierry, A., Horn, L., Von Hellermann, P., & Gardner, C. J. (2023). "No research on a dead planet": Preserving the socio-ecological conditions for academia. *Frontiers in Education, 8*, 1237076.

Thorpe, C. (2022). *Sociology in post-normal times.* Rowman & Littlefield.

Wacquant, L. J. D. (1989). For a socio-analysis of intellectuals: On "Homo Academicus." *Berkeley Journal of Sociology, 34*, 1–29.

Venugopal, R. (2015). Neoliberalism as concept. *Economy and Society, 44*(2), 165–187.

Washburn, J. (2008). *University Inc: The corporate corruption of higher education.* Basic Books.

Webb, D. (2018). Bolt-holes and breathing spaces in the system: On forms of academic resistance (or, can the university be a site of utopian possibility?). *Review of Education, Pedagogy, and Cultural Studies, 40*(2), 96–118. https://doi.org/10.1080/10714413.2018.1442081

Weller, S., & O'Neill, P. (2014). An argument with neoliberalism: Australia's place in a global imaginary. *Dialogues in Human Geography, 4*(2), 105–130.
Whelan, A. (2015). Academic critique of neoliberal academia. *Sites: A Journal of Social Anthropology and Cultural Studies, 12*(1), 130–152.

CHAPTER 4

Changing the World from the Classroom: Pedagogy as Illusio

Abstract Chapter 4 *Changing the world from the classroom: Pedagogy as illusio* explores pedagogical approaches in language teaching that have social justice aspirations. Using Basil Bernstein's (Bernstein, B. (1990). The structuring of pedagogic discourse (Vol. V: Class, Codes and Control). Routledge, London) pedagogies typology (liberal, conservative, radical, subversive) to enable systematic comparison, the chapter teases out false dichotomies that pit conservative against radical approaches, foreclosing other options. The chapter clarifies terms such as *critical* pedagogy, a term often assigned to practices that are very different despite professing a common social justice goal. The chapter provides an in-depth discussion of Critical English for Academic Purposes, and Raciolinguistics as influential manifestations of *radical* pedagogies within the field of literacy. The chapter also discusses Systemic Functional Linguistics/ Genre, Reflective Literacy and variations of Critical Literacy as examples of *subversive* pedagogies. It concludes with a means of reconciliation around concepts such as repertoire and registers, around language as a mode of critical social action, and with a call for a literacy approach that equips students with the necessary knowledge to *both* access powerful discourse and 'play the game', *and* to raise consciousness of the role of language not only in social reproduction but also in broader democratic destabilisation drives and global crises.

Keywords Social Justice · Literacy · EAP · Critical pedagogies · Liberal pedagogies · Conservative pedagogies · Radical pedagogies · Subversive pedagogies · Raciolinguistics · SFL/genre pedagogy · Repertoires · Registers · Powerful discourse

'[S]peakers lacking the legitimate competence are de facto excluded from the social domains in which this competence is required or are condemned to silence.'
Bourdieu, 1991, p. 55

Introduction

In the same way that tacit beliefs about language and ethics, teachers' pedagogies can also be implicit, acquired through experience, and ad-hoc socialisation into the teaching profession. This chapter explores pedagogical approaches in language teaching and literacy settings such as Academic Writing, English for Academic Purposes (EAP) or Teacher education. We focus specifically on the types of pedagogies that have been associated with social justice or social change and we argue that pedagogy is another facet of the illusio. We revisit decades-old debates between radical, critical, progressive and subversive approaches that have pitted different proposals that aim for different types of transformation, such as increased access, equity in outcomes, or social justice. In these debates, different problems are often conflated, terms (such as radical, critical, subversive) are often left undefined, and the label 'critical' assigned to actual different practices that only converge around a vague shared social justice goal. For some (the subversive perspective), social justice can only be attained through giving access to the codes (including revealing the linguistics/semiotics basis of achievement) in order to level the playing field for disenfranchised students. Others argue that social change, student empowerment, social justice or social transformation, requires radical change (the radical perspective). One recurrent argument hinges around a simple question: should the discourse of the powerful be taught as a matter of developing agency and enabling access, or is such teaching in fact a reproduction of systemic inequalities that enshrines linguistics variation into a discriminatory value system? This is not a question that warrants easy answers, which is probably why it is recurrent in educational debates across different countries. In fact, under different pedagogical names, progressive, radical and subversive proposals for social justice have clashed for decades (Chen & Derewianka, 2009).

This chapter aims to disentangle these threads. We use Jim Martin's (1997) adaptation for language teaching of Basil Bernstein's (1990) pedagogies typology to make visible specific criteria that can enable comparison across approaches and push beyond false dichotomies which would have us believe the choice is either to be a conservative or to be a radical educator. We then discuss and critique the approach to social justice offered by radical pedagogies, taking for example Critical EAP, and Raciolinguistics as a newer manifestation. We also discuss subversive pedagogies through examples such as Systemic Functional Linguistics/ Genre, Reflective Literacy, and variations of Critical Literacy for their strengths but also highlight some limitations. Finally, we discuss, perhaps as a means of reconciliation, the need to clarify concepts such as repertoire and registers, language as a mode of critical social action, and the need for a literacy approach that equips students with the necessary knowledge to *both* access powerful discourse to 'play the game', *and* to raise consciousness of the role of language not only in social reproduction but also in broader democratic destabilisation drives and global crises.

Pedagogy and Social Change: Teasing Out False Dichotomies

In this chapter we start with an assumption, that all educators want to make a difference (Ding, 2016). 'Education necessarily entails some kind of transformation (of students, teachers, the institution, knowledge) whenever teaching (and not just teaching) takes place. Lessons, seminars, lectures, modules, syllabi and curriculum all explicitly and implicitly aim at some notion of change, development or progress' (Ding, 2016). The type of change, and its relation to pedagogy, however, warrants a closer look. First, the range of transformation teachers want to see in their students vary from localised achievement of intended outcomes to better access to opportunities through a levelling of the playing field, or even an emancipation, the development of a broader consciousness. Educators position themselves more or less consciously on a sort of 'aspired impact cline' and this has a direct consequence on their alignment with specific pedagogies, and knowledge base. However, this complexity of goals and means to achieve them is often represented as a simplistic dichotomy that opposes an individual achievement of pragmatic learning outcomes (conservative approach) and an individual's change for social transformation (radical approaches). Terms such as radical and critical are then frequently conflated under a general social justice notion (Norton & Toohey, 2004). The abundance of recent publications in Applied Linguistics, ELT, TESOL and EAP with a Social Justice focus makes plain a yearning for change, but also attests to this ambiguity (Denis, 2023; Macrine, 2020; López-Gopar, 2018; Kukuczka, 2024; Tavares, 2024). This false dichotomy obscures the multi-dimensional complexity of situations, rarely allows for a solid social analysis of the field or the context and tends to leave key terms such as social justice ill-defined. As a result, solutions for change can be unclear, unconvincing, unfeasible or even in fact reproduce the structures and practices they profess to dismantle.

To address these questions, and tease the dichotomy apart, we need a basis on which to compare different pedagogies that aim to achieve change. We use Martin's (1999) adaptation of Bernstein's pedagogy typologies for language teaching as a starting point because of the very useful distinction between radical and subversive pedagogies as means towards change (Fig. 4.1). A key argument in this chapter is that pedagogies labelled critical in the literature can fall within a radical or subversive perspective, and therefore point to very different ontologies, practices and crucially to different potential for impact.

The typology is derived from Bernstein's (1971) concepts of framing (relative degree of control teachers and students are provided) and classification (relative boundaries between practices, between curriculum items, between agents). This cartesian plane is organised around two main pedagogical concerns: the vertical axis is a continuum between pedagogies that focus on one end on the internal, psychological, individual transformation and on the other prioritises pedagogical purpose as social transformation. The lower quadrants, radical and subversive, then, are concerned with social justice and social change. The horizontal cline distinguishes between visible pedagogies which emphasise knowledge that is made visible, and explicitly taught ('transmitted') through teacher intervention, and invisible pedagogies, which emphasise learning as 'acquiring' competence in a setting that encourages implicit, incidental learning.

The typology provides clear categories to tease out the differences between pedagogies with social justice aspirations, such as Critical EAP, Raciolinguistics or SFL/Genre pedagogy, regardless of the labels they

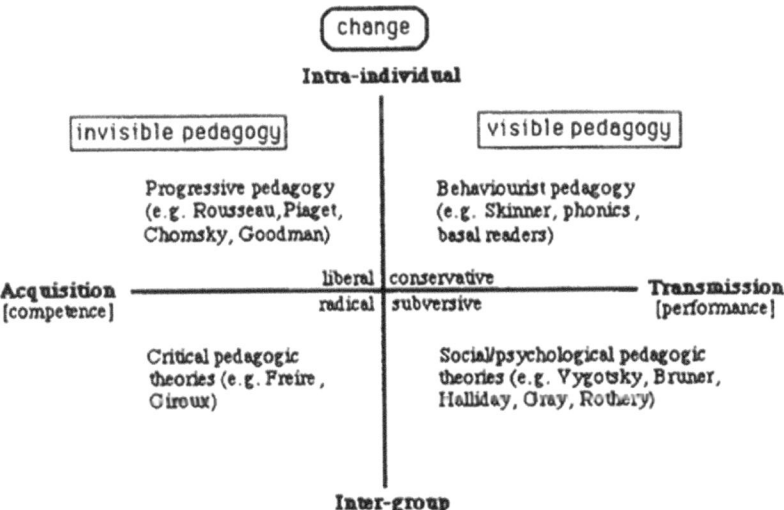

Fig. 4.1 A typology of pedagogy (Bernstein, 1990, adapted by Martin, 1997)

adopt and can, we hope, help readers evaluate various classroom enactments of these approaches around questions such as:

- What is presented as legitimate content knowledge? What is dismissed as legitimate content knowledge?
- What are the learning outcomes? Do these learning outcomes equip learners to engage in the game, to critique the game, or both?
- Is the pedagogy recommended visible or invisible? Is the basis of achievement explicitly described?
- How is criticality defined and taught? Is there a topical focus on social injustice? Are underlying principles of achievement (including linguistics) explicitly taught?

BEHAVIOURIST AND PROGRESSIVE PEDAGOGIES

In educational discussions, behaviourist pedagogies have often been dismissed as too conservative, prescriptive and too teacher-centered (Barrett & McPhail, 2023; Maton, 2014). They are part of the visible pedagogy side of the typology, but tend to rely on 'rote transmission, individualistic and exam-based competition' (Barrett & Mcphail, 2023:727). Progressive pedagogies (sometimes also called constructivist pedagogies) on the other hand, are very prominent in current higher education, and are characterised by an invisible pedagogy which Halliday described as 'benevolent inertia' (Rose & Martin, 2012, p. 30). With an invisible pedagogy, the basis of achievement, the rules of access are implicit. Progressive notions such as student-centeredness, autonomous learning and curriculum co-construction downplay teacher's direct instruction in favour of students' independent construction of their learning, and have permeated higher education discourse and practices, resulting, when misinterpreted, in an eradication of knowledge, a thinning of curriculum (Monbec, 2018; Maton, 2014; Maton & Chen, 2016; Barrett & McPhail, 2023). As Martin (1999) explains, in Australia, this meant an almost complete disappearance of knowledge about language for teachers to share with their students. This has also enabled the legitimation of the knowledge-light practitioner, itself encouraged by a neoliberal capture of higher education. This downgrading of educators' expertise is reinforced in the oft-repeated phrase 'the sage on the stage' vs 'the guide on the side', another false dichotomy, which under the guise of disparaging behaviourist or traditional pedagogies ends up legitimising teachers without expert knowledge (Barrett & McPhail, 2023). Progressive pedagogies have been bolstered by the expansion of teaching and learning centres in higher education institutions, which aim to support pedagogy, and teaching excellence, but which by their very nature and the nature of the agents who occupy them—experts in specific disciplines but rarely in education or teaching (Ding, 2022)—are disconnected from the disciplines and content knowledge and are left vulnerable to endless new fads (which are in fact 'like old wines in new bottles', Barrett & McPhail, 2023:729), barely critiqued technological innovations and the 'we must adapt!' imperative (Stiegler, 2019). Progressive approaches have been critiqued in the sciences as inefficient and generally lack convincing empirical evidence of impact (Kirschner et al., 2006). In EAP, progressive pedagogies (Communicative Language Teaching, Task-based Learning for example), have contributed to the depreciation and marginalisation of knowledge and encouraged a field which does not value teacher's expertise in their own domain (in EAP it is not rare to hear colleagues claim their area of expertise is teaching, not academic language or discourse; it is also quite common for colleagues trained in linguistics to feel their knowledge is not valued). When knowledge is undermined, expert knowers can easily be delegitimised. For subversive proponents, progressive approaches and invisible pedagogies do not provide enough knowledge, nor support and so fail students, particularly those in marginalised positions, to favour the interests of middle-class families (Rose & Martin, 2012, p.30).

RADICAL PEDAGOGIES

Radical pedagogies are located in the lower-left quadrant of Bernstein's cartesian plane. They emphasise social transformation but promote invisible pedagogy. They aim to question the relation between education and power, reveal the ways schooling reproduces dominant hegemonics (Canagarajah, 1999) and engage resistance theories to explore transformative practices (Giroux, 2001). Martin positions key radical thinkers and pedagogy experts such as Paulo Freire and Henry Giroux here (although in the literature they might be labelled *critical* as many also are in the subversive side). The two sides are very different, however, in what type of knowledge they (de)legitimise. First, radical pedagogies tend to see transformation as best achieved through using social injustice, discrimination and social issues topically, as *content knowledge*, in the classroom (Benesch, 2008; Wallace, 2003). For example, Wallace (2003) explains how Freire's pedagogy involves the learner directly in discussing their own contexts of oppression. Second, radical pedagogies tend to delegitimise field-related expert knowledge, cast as hegemonic. In literacy contexts, for example, resistance might be advocated through the active refusal to accept conventions: for example, Canagarajah (2002) advises academics to break with traditional written genres.

For these reasons, implementation of radical pedagogies can be challenging, controversial and disappointing, as they lead to an agenda that might go against teacher's values, students' self-perceptions and aspirations and because their disappearing of powerful knowledge might in fact contribute to disempowering the groups they purport to help. Wallace (2003) in her critique of Freire argues that groups labelled as 'disempowered' by researchers or educators might simply not see themselves as such or might not wish to discuss these issues in a classroom setting. Radical aspirations for change can also be used to mask a reproduction of progressivist approaches that protect the status quo. Indeed, they are on the same side of the cartesian plane as progressivists and share with these a rejection of what Freire (1996) calls the 'banking view of learning', and the transmission of knowledge seen as static. We discuss two examples of radical pedagogies below, one in EAP called Critical EAP, and versions of raciolinguistics pedagogy, which we argue is a new iteration of radical pedagogy and present similar ambiguity and weaknesses.

Critical EAP

Within English Academic Purposes, the application of radical pedagogy is mostly exemplified in Benesch's work *Critical EAP* (2008). Grounded in Paulo Freire's notion of *conscientização*, or consciousness-raising, Foucault's view of power and feminist theory (Benesch, 2008), Critical EAP aims to develop traditionally oppressed learners' agency, and enable them to contest the current conventions of their disciplines and to acknowledge traditionally undermined class, gender and race within the broader context of English global expansion. Debates in the 1990s pitted Benesch's Critical EAP, Allison's Pragmatic approaches (Allison, 1996; Johns, 1993), and Critical pragmatism coined by Pennycook (1997) who argued against what he termed 'vulgar pragmatism', a pragmatic approach which focuses on narrow practical learning outcomes, avoiding any attempt at critical engagement with the larger contexts of the academic system, and its values, norms and conventions. These debates are recurrent (often reappearing under different names, and with some variation in focus). A clear 'radical' indicator in Benesch's proposal is the emphasis on topical/thematic selection (Benesch includes anorexia, racist prejudice and migration as examples) as a means to develop students' critical thinking. Critical EAP faces critiques from those who see this as ideological imposition and a reduction of students' agency. Benesch herself acknowledges students' resistance but rationalises it as a matter of motivation, self-efficacy, autonomy and perception of relevance, missing something else which is quite plainly expressed by one of her students-participants: '*Why in all classes (I mean also in reading class) you remind us that we are immigrants?*' (quoted in Benesch, 2008, p. 123). This clearly points to the need, beyond the necessary inclusive representation in EAP materials, to focus on the *type* of representation. As we discussed in Chapter 2 in relation to the 'non-English as an L1 native speakers' label, well-intentioned inclusivity initiatives can simply reinforce the othering and deficient narratives they claim to be fighting. Merabet (2024) makes a similar argument around the 'international student' label, and Tilakaratna (2024) critiques the deficit implied in the 'Global South' label.

Another radical characteristic in Critical EAP, is the implicitness of knowledge about language (Ding & Monbec, 2024) and a vague or not mentioned language ontology which does not address issues of variation in users' repertoires and in registers, and which ignores that ideology (which these radical approaches aim to dismantle) is held up, not simply in the ideational domain, but mostly/also semiotically, through grammar and lexis (Hasan, 2005). In other words, focusing social change effort on topical issues alone, not only runs the risk of reifying students' marginalisation (as the student expresses above), but it also leaves out the powerful semiotic knowledge students need to meet their pragmatic goals, to play the game, or change the world. Recent Critical EAP initiatives, such as Ferreira's (2021) present students with the opportunity to discuss academic practices critically, but do not go into the role of language in both maintaining social structure and consciousness. The critical discussion of conventions is useful, but a limitation of Ferreira's proposal is that the approach leans on a vague language ontology which means language remains a black box. Pennycook (1997) suggests a curriculum which equips students with 'forms of linguistic, social, and cultural criticism that would be of much greater benefit to them for understanding and questioning how language works both within and outside educational institutions' (p. 263). The question remains what language ontology, what semiotic resources (including discourse and lexicogrammar, as well as multimodal resources) are taught which enables this understanding and critiquing? An approach which includes the teaching of ways lexicogrammar (including transitivity, appraisal, periodicity and engagement resources, see Chapter 7) construes the world and enacts social relations would offer a solution. If Critical EAP's mission is to raise critical consciousness, it needs more than a surface discussion of academic conventions within social contexts. It requires a language ontology that recognises the complexity of the link between language, meaning-making and consciousness and includes descriptions and teaching of language resources from social context of communication to most delicate lexicogrammar knowledge. Moreover, if it aims to maintain Freire's notion of *hope*, a heavy-handed focus on students' own marginalisation as topical content is also problematic (although we acknowledge Benesch's protest at such reduction of Critical EAP and understand that some recontextual-isations do achieve more than this when they adopt some of the subversive quadrant's principles).

Raciolinguistics

Raciolinguistics is a branch of sociolinguistics which involves unpacking the racist ideology, white supremacy and colonial heritage which, according to proponents, underlie literacy policies, curriculum and peda-gogies in the US (Flores, 2020; Rosa & Flores, 2017) and in the UK (Cushing, 2022). Raciolinguists see registers such as academic language as socially constructed within racist and colonial ideologies, which are perpetuated in literacy and language teaching in order to reproduce inequities, for example othering racialised pupils (Flores, 2020). Evidence of colonial practices surrounding literacy and language in governmental bodies such as OFSTED in the UK is documented (Acevedo, 2020; Cushing & Snell, 2023). For example, uncritiqued dichotomies between standard and non-standard registers, academic versus non-academic regis-ters, often imply a value system which places some students in a deficit position since they assume that (a) some pupils do not speak non-standard at home and (b) the non-standard register is of poorer quality. As we discuss in Chapter 2 on language ontology, teaching academic stan-dards, uncritiqued, is indeed problematic, dismissing pupils' home and community registers is abhorrent. Raciolinguists also argue that learners' repertoire characteristics are not objective but that they are shaped by the filter of whiteness and colonialism. Therefore, the lack of access or success is not due to the speakers' lack of familiarity with academic register, but rather to the way stigmatisation attaches to race and to class. For raciolin-guists, this means, for example, that adopting a standard variety register (including received pronunciation) cannot prevent racialised groups from facing rejection and discrimination (Cushing, 2023; Flores, 2020). So far, there is little to disagree with. The issue with raciolinguistics, is that these fairly well understood diagnostic statements too often lead to wholesale rejection of the teaching of academic register. We discuss below that, beyond providing an important analysis of undercurrent ideologies in school literacy programmes and policies, raciolinguistics does not present credible or even workable solutions for the classroom, partly due to a misconception of language ontology, and the role of language in social reproduction as well as ethical issues related to students' agency.

Raciolinguistics and Language Ontology

Raciolinguists emphasise the need to shift from the description of individual linguistic features to the perception of these features (Flores, 2020 p. 24). Flores critiques the dichotomy between standard and non-standard registers as flawed and as representing subjective (and racist) perceptions, rather than objective linguistic variation. Flores and Rosa (2023) argue that 'linguistic distinctions, including those between "standard" and "nonstandard" or "academic" and "social" varieties, correspond to racialized perceptions and ascriptions rather than discrete empirical patterns' (p. 425). We see this claim as related to language ontology. That these variations are perceived through subjective, racist, gendered or classis, filters is well documented, undeniable and not novel. Yet, this subjectivity in perception does not refute the objective existence of this variation. There is plenty of empirical evidence for these patterns of difference in meaning-making across different groups engaging different semiotic resources at genre, discourse and lexicogrammatical and phonological levels, and in individual repertoires (Bourdieu, 1991; Hasan, 1996). Much of Critical Discourse Analysis is devoted to highlighting these patterns of variation across contexts of communication and how they interact with class, gender, race and sustain power relations. Martin and Bednarek (2010) compile empirical studies of users' repertoire variation according to characteristics such as gender, generation, social class, nations, 'tribes' or sub-cultures. Raciolinguists clearly acknowledge the social impact of language variation, but there is little sign that they adopt linguistics theoretical underpinning that would describe this connection between actual language resources (lexicogrammar, discourse, genre), meaning-making systems, ideology, world construal, social reproduction and consciousness. In the UK, we found that this ontological vagueness means that almost any reference to *register* as academic seems to be described as ideologically discriminatory. For example, literacy approaches in UK schools, such as the *word gap*, or '*what works*' are said to be anti-Black practices which assume racialised communities as having a limited vocabulary range and where remedial vocabulary classes are disproportionally assigned to marginalised communities (Cushing, 2024). These literacy practices are seen as 'accommodation-based theories of change' which take for granted that 'language-based modifications provide the path to social justice' (Cushing & Clayton, 2024, p. 16). In Cushing's view, for example, technical or 'academic' lexis reflects a colonial ideology

(2024). As seen in Chapter 2, a language ontology such as Halliday's SFL explains that language is indeed ideological, construing worldviews and enacting power relations, but that language is also a semiotics system that evolves to serve our semiotic needs and purposes (in this case expressing abstraction, technicality, and dense disciplinary content through lexis but also through grammatical patterns such as nominalisation). As a result, while we can critique academic vocabulary as incarnating a specific worldview, this does not negate that this evolution also enables access to abstract and technical meanings and powerful disciplinary knowledge. The consequence of a raciolinguistic ideological unpicking often seems to be that the teaching of academic vocabulary, or academic registers, *itself,* is vilified. Some literacy interventions might indeed be rightfully framed as 'language correction and policing' (Acevedo, 2020; Cushing, 2022), but many, especially of the subversive type presented below offer both knowledge of powerful discourses and means to critique and act upon them.

At times, raciolinguistics proposals are more ambiguous. Flores (2020) for example, argues that pupils, while they should not be made to *master* academic language, should rather 'be language architects who are able to manipulate language for specific purposes' (p. 25). In the same paper, Flores suggests students should be provided 'opportunities to break down and analyze the language choices of speakers and writers to determine if and how they are using particular language forms for particular effect' (2020; p29). This seems to align with the subversive SFL/Genre approach we describe below, in terms of developing students' ability to understand the relation between language features choice and meaning. In fact, Flores acknowledges his lesson proposal, in the same paper, is similar to what a 'proponent of the concept of academic language' would offer and situates the difference of his proposal at the level of the teacher/educator's understanding of the legitimacy of the pupils' home language practices, which to us seems particularly rife for uncritiqued assumptions about teachers. The main issue with Flores' proposal is that without a visible acknowledgement (and teaching) of variation at genre, discourse and lexicogrammar levels (and other semiotic modalities), how students become architects of language and make these decisions, remains a mystery. The invisibility shown here places this raciolinguist approach squarely in the radical quadrant.

These contradictions constitute limitations in raciolinguistics pedagogical proposals. It is difficult to see how the dismantling of standardised linguistic categories advocated by Flores and Rosa (2015) can be done without explicitly teaching these linguistic categories. When raciolinguists are pressed on this matter, and present Audrey Lorde's misunderstood argument that one cannot dismantle the master's house with the master's tools, they disregard access to meaning-making resources as everyone's right. Language is everyone's tool. When raciolinguists clamour on social media that nothing less than a complete dismantlement of the whole oppressive educational system will do, first, we almost can hear the 1% laugh in their clubs, and second, we eagerly await their concrete plan and action to achieve this (but peer reviewed publications in standard academic English don't count!). If the proposal is the dismissal of literacy teaching of powerful discourse because it is in itself a racist act, then it is in fact disenfranchising groups further and reinforcing the power of those— the dominant classes—whose repertoire and linguistic habitus (Bourdieu, 1991) are very close to powerful registers. Raciolinguists in their proposal show they do not make the distinction between register and repertoire (we explain this in the next paragraph). To us, and as Bourdieu argues in the citation that opens the chapter, not accessing the dominant codes (both to use them and to subvert them) is a sure way to be silenced. This disagreement is decades-old and centres around the question of the role of literacy for access to dominant discourse and potential impact on social transformation, and social justice. It centres around the notion that teaching literacy is a way to level the playing field. It is by no means a simple question as we discuss in the subversive section of the chapter below.

Raciolinguistics and Sociolinguistics

Another issue we think is worth surfacing regarding raciolinguistics is that the blame for this colonial ideology is wrongly laid at the feet of scholars who described (class-based) variation, particularly Basil Bernstein who, perhaps for his ill-choice of name for repertoire variation patterns he observed in children from different social classes, namely *restricted* for working class, and *elaborated* for middle class, is vilified (Hasan, 2005). In Bernstein's time, and ever since, his ideas have been misread, misrepresented for simply pointing out 'the persistence of structural educational inequalities' (Hasan, 2005; Mueller, 2004, p. 1). Bernstein deserves a much more careful reading. The notion that Bernstein inspired 'gap ideologies', realised as pedagogical practices such as vocabulary drills and grammatical drills is further evidence of a general misunderstanding of his work (and still does not evidence Bernstein's ideology as discriminatory). Working closely with social semiotics linguists such as Ruqaiya Hasan, who empirically showed what class-based patterns of variation looks like at lexicogrammatical level, Bernstein was keenly aware of users' semiotic variation's impact on attainment in a system that devalued marginalised working-class students (Bartlett, 2017). Despite raciolinguists' claims, Bernstein did not attach an intrinsic value to the different codes nor did he encourage an 'accommodationist' approach to literacy (Cushing, 2022). Codes are an invisible element of communication, linked to (self) positioning in the social space, to predispositions to meaning, to what each of us sees as relevant and as possible for us to say in a given social context, and this is influenced by a range of factors including class, race, gender and generation (Hasan, 2005). Bernstein is not classist, nor is he racist. He simply argued, as Bourdieu (1991) did, that language repertoires (habitus or coding orientation) have a deep influence on school attainment, and so on social reproduction and that while all different codes are legitimate, 'the socio -economic institutions of the middle-classes ensure that one and only one of these fashions of speaking, namely their own, affirms the values -the orientation to meaning- which are invariably associated with what counts as success in the macro-community' (Hasan, 1996, p. 34). In raciolinguistics literature, as far as we can tell, the difference between the notions of codes, repertoires and register is ignored. Yet, they are not synonymous. Codes and repertoires concern variation among users, while register concerns variation among texts (Martin, 2010). Repertoires are characteristics of the individual's language resources. On the other hand, registers do not concern the individual's repertoire, but consist of description of expected discursive patterns (at genre, semantics and lexicogrammar levels) in specific contexts (schooling, academic, disciplines...). As Systemic Functional Semiotics has shown, registers are affected by independent factors such as the subject matter (field), the situation, the participants role (tenor), the mode of discourse and the medium of discourse (mode) (Hasan, 2005, p. 177). It seems that the raciolinguist literature discussed in this section tends to confuse literacy aimed at developing familiarity with registers as an attempt to police repertoires (which it can be, but the discussion must acknowledge and address the difference).

Critics and criticisms of Bernstein need a critical reading too. Indeed, Martin (1997) analysing the reactions to Bernstein's ideas—namely the recognition that semantic variation has educational implications which underpin social reproduction of class distinction—sees this dismissal as an attempt to maintain the schooling advantage for the middle classes (Martin, 1997) and a reflection of a liberal perception of people's differences as incompatible with their understanding of equality (Martin, 2010). For Hasan (2005, p. 43), the virulence of the attacks has always been proportionate to its lack of substance. For example, critics of Bernstein often ignore the literacy programmes aiming at redistributing semiotics resources that his ideas motivated (the Sydney School pedagogy, and Kalantsis' Multiliteracies programme are examples). They mostly criticise him for the lack of empirical validity and accuse him of classism or racism. Neither of these attacks survive any serious engagement with Bernstein's work. It seems to us that raciolinguists would benefit from revisiting the work of such a strong ally in the quest for social change. In fact, recent raciolinguist and anti-racist literacy work in the US is revisiting Bernstein and Halliday, for the powerful combination of social theory and social linguistics (Mizell & Accurso, 2023; also see Ramirez, 2020 for his discussion of raciolinguists and pedagogical proposal). Mizell (2022) emphasises agency for example when he states that 'even though racialized and otherwise minoritized communities will not be 'saved' by learning how to approximate dominant structures, what can happen when they explicitly know how language is constructed and often used against them and sometimes for them, they can make explicit choices regarding how they want to fight and how they want to position themselves' (p. 8).

Raciolinguistics, Learner's Agency and Ethics

Finally, we will raise ethical issues in some raciolinguistics' pedagogical proposals. First, the representation of whole communities as racialised or working class (or in higher education as 'international') is a reductive and essentialist view of groups that are diverse in many more ways than the label 'racialised' or 'working-class' or 'international' allows (Merabet, 2024; Wallace, 2003). While this homogenisation reduces the variety in these groups, the emphasis on selected commonalities contributes to minimise disadvantages related to poverty and access (Wallace, 2003). This homogenisation tends to serve the reification of a deficit narrative, representing communities as agentless, casting whole groups as victims. For those who see language as a powerful tool that construes the world and people's identities, and that positions them within it, as was shown in Chapter 2 on language ontology, this is particularly uncomfortable.

This discomfort is reinforced when arguments against teaching powerful genres and discourse are written in exactly the standard academic register which is denied to these communities, and which, incidentally, has allowed these academics to gather recognition and rewards. Martin, faced with a similar discussion in Australia in the 1980s, commented that 'as agents of symbolic control, we [academics], have no right *not* to make our genres available to anyone who wants them, since if Aboriginal people are to directly negotiate their future in Australia they will need to control these discourses' (1997, p. 420). Martin and Rose see the argument as disingenuous:

> The [...] observation we would make as far as genre and power is concerned has to do with the discourse of critique itself and who has access to it. We have always found it an instructive exercise to take the language of critical theory and compare it with the language of the disempowered voices it purports to speak for. Who, we wonder, will teach this discourse to the other, if we listen to the critical theorists and stop teaching powerful genres and the language that realises them? Or are we being called upon to imagine a utopian plenum in which abstract discourse is not required and alternative discourses, enjoying equal status one to another, abound?
> Martin & Rose (2008, pp. 259-260)

As was found with Critical EAP, raciolinguists also propose to introduce racial discrimination as topical content within literacy provisions. Flores (2020) argues for 'a systematic incorporation of the structural barriers confronting racialized communities into the solutions we propose'. Without any intention to reject this proposal, we think it raises the same questions we asked of Critical EAP: what type of discrimination is surfaced, why and how? How does this impact learners' worldview, their right to build their identity through their varied attributes, dispositions, and talents, rather than as identified narrowly, or as a reaction to discrimination? In these proposals, are traditionally marginalised groups represented *as marginalised* in classroom materials? What is the role of parents within decisions made about classroom activities and focus? Some proposals put forward by teachers consist of useful discussions around language discrimination which have their place in schools at appropriate ages (also to be discussed), but they are not literacy development activities per se (see Thea in Cushing, 2023, for example). Cushing admits that the teachers he worked with experienced pressure from *parents* (p. 7), not just from school managements intent on enforcing OFSTED ill-designed literacy approaches. What are we to make of parents' reluctance? Is it linked to an insistence their children should receive the same education as all other children? Might they feel that a label assigned to their children will shape their self-conception (Appiah, 2005)? This should warn educators and academics that they need a degree of humility and a recognition that they may not have the necessary wisdom to build criticality in learners without limiting them, defining who they are and reifying the deficit views they aim to counter. We find some of the proposals on the radical side too essentialising, and divisive around identity markers which incapacitates solidarity across differences, and are, in fact, too violent for teachers to implement.

Unearthing discriminatory ideologies that underlie educational approaches is essential work (see Ding & Monbec, 2024 for an analysis of this in English for Academic Purposes) and raciolinguistics has much to offer in this analysis. Pedagogical solutions, however, are much more difficult to devise and we believe that raciolinguistics will need to contend with language ontology including the distinction between repertoire and register variation, with learner agency and ethics more than it has so far.

SUBVERSIVE PEDAGOGIES

In Bernstein's typology, subversive pedagogies aim for social transformation as radical pedagogies do, but share with traditional pedagogies an explicit transmission of powerful knowledge and visible pedagogy. Approaches such as Critical Literacy, Reflection Literacy from Hasan, Cope and Kalantziz's Multiliteracy pedagogy, and the Sydney School Genre Pedagogy are examples. Influenced by Hallidayan linguistics, the Sydney School Genre pedagogy was devised to counter progressivist agenda in literacy in schools which, as we saw, favours a non-interventionist approach (Wallace, 2003). These models emphasise explicit instruction of the linguistic forms, the 'powerful genres' that provide access to dominant discourse (Cope & Kalantzis, 1993). This means that literacy and textual access are seen as part of systemic gatekeeping (Martin & Rose, 2005), and variation in meaning-making is integral to the role of language in the constitution of social structure (Hasan, 2005). As Luke explains, the learner here is not the 'revolutionary, transformative agent conceptualised by Freire but rather one with enhanced individual agency' (Luke, 1997). This agency is built through the explicit teaching of choice over semiotics systems, including linguistic features. Subversive pedagogies such as SFL/Genre, or Cope and Kalantzis' (1993) work then lean on a clear functional ontology, a comprehensive theory of language, a social semiotics view of language in learning processes and a socio constructivist approach to learning. In this section, we focus on critique. In Chapter 6, we detail what a subversive approach can look like in curriculum and classroom practice.

Subversive pedagogies are not immune to criticism. As Martin (1997) explains, subversive pedagogies can be discursively constructed as reactionary, not radical enough for some, 'using the masters' tools' and as too radical for others since they aim to give access to powerful codes, develop agency and challenge power. Referring to these struggles in Australia in the 1980s, Martin says 'It was a little unnerving to be construed by the left as right and by the right as left, often in the course of a single day!' (1997, p. 419). These criticisms are worth revisiting.

First, a recurrent criticism of the SFL/Genre model is its lack of effectiveness for social change. Critics argue that an emphasis on the direct transmission of genres does not necessarily lead to a critical analysis of that genre, but may simply consolidate genres as hegemonic (Lee, 1993). It is true that a subversive approach can be delivered with a focus on technical linguistic features, forgetting potential to critique. Recontextualisation of SFL into pedagogy can treat text as post-mortem (O'Donnell, 2013) or swap formal labels for functional ones without reflecting the underlying ontology. Any work of recontextualisation from a theory to classroom practice can distort original intent, but we would argue that subversive approaches, by their focus on explicit interventionist approaches are less susceptible to this distortion than the radical side of the quadrant.

Second, the link between literacy and power is questioned. Luke (1997) argues this link is assumed to be linear within SFL/Genre approaches. For him, power is not inherent in genres, but rather 'power is utterly sociologically contingent' (Luke, 1997). Wallace (2003) agrees that 'power is not so readily transmitted or handed over from powerful to less powerful groups' (p. 60). Other, material, gatekeeping structures keep power in the hands of some, regardless of whether one learns the powerful genres that operate. This echoes valid arguments put forward in radical pedagogies. To these reservations, we would also add that teaching the codes is more likely to foster assimilation or social mobility than social change.

Finally, as we saw above with the discussion on raciolinguistics, the act of teaching powerful genres is sometimes framed as reinforcing hegemonic discourse and discrimination and as further devaluing the discourse of marginalised groups. Within a social semiotics view of language and a subversive view of pedagogy, however, there is a wide agreement that access to meaning-making is seen as a way to develop agency (or at least to have a fairer chance at playing or changing the game), and that genres need to be familiar before they can be manipulated or contested (Bahktin, 2010; Halliday, 1996; Martin, 1997). The solution can never be to withhold what is already unfairly distributed powerful discourse or powerful knowledge. The more explicitly the discourse of the powerful is taught, the more students are given the opportunity to make decisions for themselves, use the discourse if it suits their purpose, discard it, or subvert it. Schools and teachers can very well both value their pupils' home registers and teach powerful genres. 'Learning one discourse need not efface another' (Martin, 1997: 420).

CONCLUSION: REGISTERS, REPERTOIRES AND RECONCILIATION

In this chapter, we have critiqued different pedagogical approaches that share social justice aspirations. The subversive side has the advantage that in showing the codes, and making powerful language explicit, it preserves students' agency. It acknowledges that while all repertoires are equally legitimate and apt, not all repertoires are equal in their socioeconomic and political weight. Whether subversive pedagogies do lead to social transformation rather than simply assimilation is not completely clear. On the other hand, the radical approaches that erase powerful knowledge present significant issues in applicability, but also ethically in their reduction of student agency, and their reification of deficit narratives.

Pennycook (1997) argues that the need to critique and the need to give people access to conventions is 'a classic tension in critical approaches to education' (p. 266) and argues 'we do not need to see this as a dichotomous choice [...] but instead can work with both'. We see much of the disagreement as related to different conceptualisation of language, in particular the understanding of repertoire and register variation and their relation to power. We all function in different registers every day and adjust our linguistic selections according to the context and the goal of communication. Understanding the difference between repertoires and registers, enables us to see register variation as a legitimate goal of literacy programmes, and can help dismiss the notion that learning to use different registers is discriminatory of individuals' repertoires. While it may be true that mastery of the dominant discourse does not necessarily lead to the obtention of power (as Luke argued), in the same way, encouraging people to change their attitudes towards non powerful discourses will not have the wished outcome, because the relation between powerful discourse and language is not arbitrary (Martin, 1997). On the other hand, when social justice is defined as *increasing agency* without assuming all learners labelled marginalised have the same experiences, or aspirations, and when language is taught as a social semiotic system, a middle ground might be found that preserves both critical potency, powerful knowledge and learner agency. In particular, the social realist concept of 'radical visible pedagogy' drawn from Bernstein (Barrett & McPhail, 2023) and literacy-based proposals such as Kartika-Ningsih and Rose (2018), Ramírez & Gutiérrez (2023), Ramirez (2020, 2023, Forthcoming) and Guerra-Lyons and Mendinueta (2020) are promising.

Reconciliation might reside there.

The questions we raise are not easy to answer (for us in any case) but we hope the chapter achieves at least a problematisation of social justice pedagogies and presents a critique that sets them as part of the illusio or 'the enchanted circle of collective denial' (Bourdieu, 2000, p. 5). We hope the chapter can equip educators with useful tools to question pedagogies presented to them (sometimes in the form of social media monoglossic aphorisms) as transformative, radical, critical, subversive or progressive so they can analyse these proposals and their own practices with student agency as a core concern in the type of transformation they aspire to contribute to.

REFERENCES

Acevedo, M. C. (2020). *Bringing language to consciousness: Teacher professional learning in genre-based reading pedagogy* [PhD Thesis]. Open University (United Kingdom).

Allison, D. (1996). Pragmatist discourse and English for academic purposes. *English for Specific Purposes, 15*(2), 85–103.

Appiah, K. A. (2005). *The ethics of identity*. Princeton University Press.

Bakhtin, M. M. (2010). *Speech genres and other late essays*. University of Texas Press.

Barrett, B., & McPhail, G. (2023). Conceptualizing a radical visible pedagogy. *Journal of Education, 203*(3), 726–735.

Bartlett, T. (2017). Context in systemic functional linguistics: Towards scalar supervenience? In T. Bartlett & G. O'Grady (Eds.), *The Routledge handbook of systemic functional linguistics* (pp. 399–414). Routledge.

Bednarek, M., & Martin, J. R. (Eds.). (2010). *New discourse on language: Functional perspectives on multimodality, identity, and affiliation.* Continuum.

Benesch, S. (2008). *Critical English for academic purposes: Theory, politics, and practice.* Lawrence Erlbaum. https://doi.org/10.1016/j.jeap.2008.09.002

Bernstein, B. (1971). *Class, codes and control: Theoretical studies towards a sociology of language* (Vol. I). Routledge.

Bernstein, B. (1990). *The structuring of pedagogic discourse (Vol. V: Class, Codes and Control)*. Routledge.

Bernstein, B. (1996). *Pedagogy, symbolic control and identity: Theory, research, critique.* Taylor & Francis.

Bourdieu, P. (1991). *Language and symbolic power (J. B. Thompson, Ed.).* Polity Press.

Bourdieu, P. (2000). *Pascalian meditations.* Stanford University Press.

Canagarajah, A. S. (1999). *Resisting linguistic imperialism in English teaching.* Oxford University Press.

Canagarajah, A. S. (2002). *A geopolitics of academic writing.* University of Pittsburgh Press.

Chen, H., & Derewianka, D. (2009). Binaries and beyond: A Bernsteinian perspective on change in literacy education. *Research Papers in Education, 24*(2), 223–245. https://doi.org/10.1080/02671520902867226

Cope, B., & Kalantzis, M. (1993). Introduction: How a genre approach to literacy can transform the way writing is taught. In B. Cope & M. Kalantzis (Eds.), *The powers of literacy: A genre approach to teaching writing* (pp. 1–21). The Falmer Press.

Cushing, I. (2022). *Standards, stigma, surveillance: Raciolinguistic ideologies and England's schools.* Springer Nature.

Cushing, I. (2023). A raciolinguistic perspective from the United Kingdom. *Journal of Sociolinguistics., 27*(5), 473–477.

Cushing, I. (2024). Tiered vocabulary and raciolinguistic discourses of deficit: From academic scholarship to education policy. *Language and Education.* https://doi.org/10.1080/09500782.2024.2308824

Cushing, I., & Clayton, D. (2024). Teachers challenging language discrimination in England's schools: A typology of resistance. *Journal of Language, Identity & Education.* https://doi.org/10.1080/15348458.2024.2354478

Cushing, I., & Snell, J. (2023). The (white) ears of Ofsted: A raciolinguistic perspective on the listening practices of the school inspectorate. *Language in Society, 52*(3), 363–386. https://doi.org/10.1017/S0047404522000094

Deniz, O. H. (2023). *Social justice and the language classroom: Reflection, action, and transformation.* Edinburgh University Press.

Ding, A. (2016). EAP as pharmakon: Are we all neoliberals now? https://teachingeap.wordpress.com/2016/02/19/eap-as-pharmakon-are-we-all-neoliberals-now/

Ding, A. (2022). Bourdieu and field analysis: EAP and its practitioners. In A. Ding & M. Evans (Eds.), *Social theory for English for academic purposes: Foundations and perspectives.* Bloomsbury.

Ding, A., & Monbec, L. (2024). A socio-analysis of English for academic purposes. In A. Ding & L. Monbec (Eds.), *Practitioner agency and identity in English for academic purposes.* Bloomsbury.

Flores, N. (2020). From academic language to language architecture: Challenging raciolinguistic ideologies in research and practice. *Theory into Practice, 59*(1), 22–31.

Flores, N., & Rosa, J. (2015). Undoing appropriateness: Raciolinguistic ideologies and language diversity in education. *Harvard Educational Review, 85*(2), 149–171.

Flores, N., & Rosa, J. (2023). Undoing raciolinguistics. *Journal of Sociolinguistics, 27,* 421–427. https://doi.org/10.1111/josl.12643

Ferreira, M. M. (2021). Using developmental teaching to promote critical EAP in an academic writing course in English. In C. MacDiarmid & J. MacDonald (Eds.), *Pedagogies in English for academic purposes: Teaching and learning in international contexts* (pp. 75–106). Bloomsbury.

Freire, P. (1996). *Pedagogy of the oppressed (revised).* Continuum.

Giroux, H. A. (2001). *Theory and resistance in education: Towards a pedagogy for the opposition.* Bergin & Garvey.

Guerra-Lyons, J. D., & Mendinueta, N. R. (2020). On the notion of "owning a forest": Ideological awareness and Genre-based Pedagogy in university critical literacy. *DELTA: Documentação De Estudos Em Lingüística Teórica e Aplicada, 36*(4), 2020360412.

Halliday, M. A. K. (1996). Literacy and linguistics: A functional perspective. In R. Hasan & G. Williams (Eds.), *Literacy in society* (pp. 308–338). Longman.

Hasan, R. (1996). Ways of saying, ways of meaning. In C. Cloran, D. Butt, & G. Williams (Eds.), *Ways of saying, ways of meaning* (pp. 191–242). Cassell.

Hasan, R. (2005). *Language society and consciousness. J. Webster (Ed.)* (Vol. 1). Equinox.

Johns, A. M. (1993). Too much on our plates: A response to Terry Santos. *Journal of Second Language Writing, 2*(1), 83–88.

Kartika-Ningsih, H., & Rose, D. (2018). Language shift: Analysing language use in multilingual classroom interactions. *Functional Linguistics, 5*(1), 1–22.

Kirschner, P. A., Sweller, J., & Clark, R. E. (2006). Why minimal guidance during instruction does not work: An analysis of the failure of constructivist, discovery, problem-based, experiential, and inquiry-based teaching. *Educational Psychologist, 41*(2), 75–86.

Kukuczka, J. (2024). Curriculum for change. In P. Breen & M. Le Roux (Eds.), *Social justice in EAP and ELT contexts: Global higher education perspectives* (pp. 39–56).

Lee, C. D. (1993). *Signifying as a scaffold for literary interpretation: The pedagogical implications of an African American discourse genre*. National Council of Teachers of English.

López-Gopar, M. E. (Ed.). (2018). *International perspectives on critical pedagogies in ELT*. Springer.

Luke, A. (1997). Genres of power: Literacy education and the production of capital. In R. Hasan & G. Williams (Eds.), *Literacy in society* (pp. 308–338). Longman.

Macrine, S. L. (Ed.). (2020). *Critical pedagogy in uncertain times: Hope and possibilities*. Springer Nature.

Martin, J. R. (1997). Linguistics and the consumer: Theory in practice. *Linguistics and Education, 9*(4), 409–446.

Martin, J. R. (2010). Semantic variation: Modelling realisation, instantiation and individuation in social semiosis. In M. Bednarek & J. R. Martin (Eds.), *New discourse on language: Functional perspectives on multimodality, identity, and affiliation* (pp. 1–34). Continuum.

Martin, J. R., & Rose, D. (2005). Designing literacy pedagogy: Scaffolding democracy in the classroom. In R. Hasan, C. M. I. M. Matthiessen, & J. Webster (Eds.), *Continuing discourse on language: A functional perspective* (pp. 251–280). Equinox.

Maton, K. (2014). *Knowledge and knowers: Towards a realist sociology of education*. Routledge.

Maton, K., & Chen, R. T. (2016). Specialization from Legitimation code theory: How the basis of achievement shapes student success. In R. Martin, Jim, K. Maton, P. Wang, & Z. Wang (Eds.), *Understanding Academic Discourse* (pp. 1–22). Shanghai Jiao Tong University.

Merabet, R. (2024). Students we label international: An urgent call to reconceptualise research with international students. *Equality, Diversity and Inclusion*, Vol. ahead-of-print No. ahead-of-print. https://doi.org/10.1108/EDI-01-2024-0048

Monbec, L. (2018). Designing an EAP curriculum for transfer: A focus on knowledge. *Journal of Academic Language and Learning, 12*(2), A88–A101.

Mizell, J. D. (2022). Culturally sustaining systemic functional linguistics: Towards an explicitly anti-racist and anti-colonial languaging and literacy pedagogy. *Linguistics and Education, 72,* 101108.

Mizell, J. D., & Accurso, K. (2023). Reckoning with race in North American genre pedagogy. *Journal of Literacy Innovation, 8*(3), 3–11.

Muller, J., Davies, B., & Morais, A. (Eds.). (2004). *Reading Bernstein, researching Bernstein.* RoutledgeFalmer.

Norton, B., & Toohey, K. (Eds.). (2004). *Critical pedagogies and language learning.* Cambridge University Press.

O'Donnell, M. (2013). A dynamic view of choice in writing: Composition as text evolution. In L. Fontaine, T. Bartlett, & G. O'Grady (Eds.), *Systemic functional linguistics: Exploring choice* (pp. 247–266). Cambridge University Press.

Pennycook, A. (1997). Vulgar pragmatism, critical pragmatism, and EAP. *English for Specific Purposes, 16*(4), 253–269.

Ramírez, A. (2020). The case for culturally and linguistically relevant pedagogy: Bilingual reading to learn for Spanish-speaking immigrant mothers. *System, 95,* 102379.

Ramírez, A. (2023). A bilingual path towards undoing linguistic imperialism in English language teaching. *Journal of Literacy Innovation, 8*(3), 73–89.

Ramírez, A. (Forthcoming). *Genre-based pedagogical translanguaging: Classroom discourse and design.* Bloomsbury.

Ramírez, A., & Gutiérrez, G. (2023). Bilingual reading to learn for emergent to advanced bilingual latina immigrant mothers in the United States. In C. Acevedo, D. Rose, & Whittaker, R. (Eds.), *Reading to learn, reading the world: How genre-based literacy pedagogy is democratizing education.* Equinox.

Rose, D., & Martin, J. R. (2012). *Learning to write, reading to learn: Genre, knowledge and pedagogy in the Sydney School.* Equinox.

Rosa, J., & Flores, N. (2017). Unsettling race and language: Toward a raciolinguistic perspective. *Language in Society, 46*(5), 621–647.

Stiegler, B. (2019). *Il faut s'adapter.* Gallimard.

Tavares, V. (Ed.). (2024). *Social justice through pedagogies of multiliteracies: Developing and strengthening L2 learner agency and identity.* Taylor & Francis.

Tilakaratna, N. L. (2024). EAP practitioners in the global south: Participation, positioning and agency in the context of 'peripheral scholars and scholarship. In A. Ding & L. Monbec (Eds.), *Practitioner agency and identity in English for academic purposes* (pp. 67–87). Bloomsbury.

Wallace, C. (2003). *Critical reading in language education.* Springer.

PART II

Recovery

Heresy, Ethics and Scholarship

Abstract Chapter 5, Heresy, Ethics and Scholarship, focuses on '*doing something*' *within* language education in universities. The chapter draws, specifically, on our own field English for Academic Purposes (EAP) and develops an *ethics* for language educators. Starting from the need to conduct socio-analyses as groundwork for change, the chapter details a socio-analysis of the field of EAP which illuminates forms of injustices and domination. It argues this can trigger an informed and collective response by revealing potential choices and possibilities for the future—a form of heresy. The chapter sees scholarship as central to this ethics and redefines it as broader than SoTL, and free from neoliberal imperatives that plague research. This ethics also requires engaging critically with agents in the field. Finally, this ethics argues for a developed knowledge base that allows practitioners a potent specialism and role within universities. In EAP, this means making visible the entanglements of academic communication within disciplinary epistemological and social forces to disciplinary colleagues and students, with potential (ethical) changes in disciplinary communication practices in teaching, research, and policies and practices.

Keywords EAP · Language Teaching · Ethics · Socio-analysis · Heresy · Scholarship · Knowledge base · Reflexivity · Negative ethics

L. Monbec and A. Ding, *Recovering Language in Higher Education*, https://doi.org/10.1007/978-3-031-76699-2_5

Moving beyond dark academe is only possible through the production of an alternative to capitalism—without it, the rotting corpse of dark academe is the lot of higher education in the twenty-first century.

Di Leo, 2024: 212.

Most people find it easier to imagine the end of the world than the end of capitalism.
Stypinska, 2020: 2.
For those with a perceptive eye, what can be seen in the 'large' can also be seen in the small
Leibniz (1714)

INTRODUCTION

It is difficult not to feel resentment. Resentment that, despite what appears overwhelming evidence that the intellectual argument has been won (Collini, 2012), despite considerable empirical evidence that academics are deeply unhappy (Erickson et al., 2021), despite a clearly dysfunctional and destructive neoliberal university that serves only the very few, despite *everything*, the onus is on those that oppose the current ideology and practices within universities and beyond to provide solutions. Those who endorse, support, contribute and profit from neoliberal universities do not have to justify their actions nor listen to complaints. This resentment is doubled: 'the effect of these arguments and objections on those who make and implement policies for universities has been … all but invisible' (Collini, 2012: 116). There is a flippant arrogance when they do comment:

> There is a comforting tale that heads of higher education institutions (HEIs) like to tell each other. 'Go around your university or college,' they say, 'and ask the first ten people who you meet how their morale is. The response will always be "rock-bottom." Then ask them what they are working on. The responses will be full of life, of optimism and of enthusiasm for the task in hand.
> Watson, 2009: 169.

Despite this resentment, despite frustrations with both the cynical appropriation of and profiting from discontent with neoliberalism by some academics and the propagation of cruel utopias which blight rather than inspire hope, we are condemned to *do something*. That *something* is the focus of this chapter. We will not offer an erudite, essayist, wistful, nostalgic or ironic contemplation of the state of higher education. We do not have the symbolic, social or cultural capital to be taken seriously even if we tried. Nor will we offer a utopia, a manifesto or a blistering condemnation. There is a very crowded market for these and we could not add much that is useful. What we will offer in this chapter is instead a more limited and focused account of what can be done *within* language education in universities. We will draw, specifically, on our own field (EAP) and we hope readers operating in adjacent fields in higher education will be able to extract some benefit from our analysis.

In order to provide an account, we will return to Bourdieu to frame and develop an ethics for language educators. We are *not* trading on any capital we might accrue through alignment with Bourdieu, nor are we part of a 'ecclesiastic semisecret society' (Hobbis & Hobbis, 2013: 448), nor part of a 'cargo cult' of Bourdieu scholars (idem:450). Nor, indeed, are we ventriloquising Bourdieu or writing behind the mask of Bourdieu to give us gravitas and, by association, cultural capital. Nor are we delegating to Bourdieu our thoughts. Instead, the concepts Bourdieu developed, especially for the purposes of this chapter, such as socio-analysis, reflexivity and illusio help us to have:

> a small chance of knowing what game we play and of minimizing the ways in which we are manipulated by the forces of the field in which we evolve . . . [Sociology] allows us to discern the sites where we do indeed enjoy a degree of freedom and those where we do not.
> Bourdieu & Wacquant, 1992: 198–9.

Our starting point, then, is to acknowledge, and share, Bourdieu's *disillusion*, although 'liable to appear self-destructive' (Bourdieu, 2000: 7) nonetheless, we will argue, offers a heretical symbolic transgression that opens up rather than closes down the future.

HERETICAL SOCIO-ANALYSIS

In this section, we very succinctly outline the salient field of English for Academic Purposes through a sketch of a socio-analysis. This lays the groundwork for establishing an ethics for language educators in the following section.

Our first assertion is that EAP is liable to permanent *crisis* because as a field it is ill-defined and porous:

> Because these posts ill-defined and ill-guaranteed but open and 'full of potential' as the phrase goes, leave their occupants the possibility of defining them by bringing the embodied necessity which is constitutive of their habitus, their future depends on what is made of them by their occupants, or at least those of them who, in the struggles with the 'profession' and in confrontations with neighbouring and rival professions, manage to impose the definition of the profession most favourable to what they are. Bourdieu, 2000: 158.

There are no 'sufficiently high entry barriers' (Bourdieu, 2000: 111) to enter EAP. Qualifications and credentials to enter the field as practitioners are unclear and confusing (cf Ding and Campion (2016), Ding (2019) Ding and Bruce (2017), Ding (2022) and Ding and Monbec (2024) for a more detailed account of the position and status of practitioners). As such, generally EAP practitioners enter and operate within the field of EAP with highly diminished cultural capital (intellectual and academic capitals) resulting in a highly subservient position within the larger HE field. This has profound consequences for their power, agency and symbolic capital. EAP centres or units, often positioned and run as a service (with commercial obligations to make a profit) rather than an academic endeavour, exist 'in the zones of uncertainty in social space' (MacDonald, 2016), and can be located in business schools, central services, academic schools or as independent units. EAP has no obvious home. Private providers, who provide profits to shareholders, operate aggressively to take over university EAP provision and have been extremely successful in doing so. Senior university leaders are easily seduced by corporate promises of increasing the 'pipeline' (suggestive of crude oil) of lucrative 'international students' who provide considerable wealth to the universities and to the providers themselves, while at the same time enabling the elimination of university-funded practitioners and centres (and those practitioners made redundant may be reemployed by the private provider earning less, with a limited pension, limited workers' rights, and few opportunities to progress and develop). Those practitioners that remain in universities have an array of nomenclature and contractual statuses, including highly precarious ones, as well as largely limited opportunities for promotion, reward and recognition. EAP is condemned to the edge of academia and always susceptible to tipping over the edge and out of sight completely.

Agents within the field have compounded this crisis, for example BALEAP (British Association of Lecturers of English for Academic Purposes) in their passivity in relation to privatisation of EAP where it was:

> evident the lack of any collective policies or positions by BALEAP as an organisation on the issue of privatization. Although appeals from members for information and support have occurred over the 20+ year period of the list, there has been no attempt by BALEAP to establish any working group, organisational repository or clearing house where information about the processes of privatization (or outsourcing), the companies involved, their strategies, policies and failings, (and crucially, their effects on the working lives of BALEAP members) could have been documented.
> Ding, Bruce and Bond (2022: 10).

Because of its porous nature, EAP as a field is liable to intense struggles over claims to legitimacy and power. Practitioners are liable to engage in defining the field in ways 'most favourable to what they are'. Many are comfortable with, or at least resigned to, a service and mercantile role, many directors (and colleagues) discourage or disparage scholarship and many practitioners refuse to engage with scholarship and research. Many claim that they have linguistic or pedagogical capital. Many seek and obtain managerial roles and power without much academic or intellectual capital, and many do not see EAP as anything other than an 'industry'. Far from all though.

There appears to be a flourishing field of research in EAP and celebratory disciplinary claims for EAP have been made by those with luminary status (cf. Hyland, 2012, Hamp-Lyons, 2011). Yet systematic reviews of the EAP research literature (Hyland & Jiang, 2021; Liu & Hu, 2021; Riazi et al., 2020) indicate that practitioners are very poorly served by research in EAP. Journals tend to narrow their focus over time with a reduced and reductive coverage of the field (for an extended discussion see Bruce, 2021) representing 'a rupture with practitioners, practice and pedagogy where claims of pedagogical implications are often unjustified' (Ding, 2022: 161. See also Bruce, 2021: 26). Similar observations have also been made about pedagogical implications of EAP research by Swales

(2019) and Cheng (2019). Researchers in EAP are subject to all the pressures to publish outlined in Chapter 3 and, consequently, it is legitimate to question the meaningfulness of much of what is researched and published. It is those who have sufficient capitals who can and do define and shape the ideational field of EAP. There is a clear rupture between the EAP research field and its practitioners (Ding, 2022).

We (Ding & Monbec, 2024) undertook a socio-analysis of EAP and our main findings can be summarised as follows:

> We established a fracture or rupture between EAP as a discipline and EAP as a field of practice. Who is significant in each of these fields is not or is no longer synonymous. What is valued and not valued in the field by practitioners emerged as contested, and the field's ethics remains remarkably unreflexive, focusing on the behaviour of others rather than a sensitivity to what practitioners, as agents, might be able to enact/embody. Ethics was also disconnected from what practitioners perceive as their potential contributions to the field. These contributions read as highly orthodox and focused on a knowledge of language which, while moving away from prescriptivist form and accuracy, still seems limited in terms of connection with its social and political context and still portrays EAP as limited in terms of the range of semiotic systems it encompasses.
> Ding & Monbec, 2024: 37-38.

Our impetus for conducting this socio-analysis of EAP, which aims at identifying and challenging the social and political unconscious that undermines the objectivity of knowledge, was because of a sense of crisis in EAP—both existential and ethical—and a need to a break with practices *within* and doxas *about* the field, Doxa is 'a set of fundamental beliefs which do not even need to be asserted in the form of an explicit, self-conscious dogma' (Bourdieu, 2000: 16). We wanted to break 'the enchanted circle of collective denial' (idem: 2000: 5). Moreover, as *heterodox* agents in the field of EAP and within the university (perhaps especially so), we felt the fate of all those who are dominated in a field:

> obliged to wait for everything to come from others, from the holders of power over the game, and the objective and subjective prospect of gain that it can offer, being masters at playing on the anxiety that inevitably arises from the tension between the intensity of the expectancy and the improbability of its being satisfied.
> Bourdieu, 2000: 237.

Any socio-analysis is also an *auto-analysis* and much of our work, together, with others, and drawing on those who share a sense of disarticulation and anomie in EAP, can be seen as motivated by not only wanting to break 'the enchanted circle of collective denial' but also to break with the holders of power over the game, to break with the illusio, and to redirect the intensity of expectancy to break the improbability of its being satisfied. Rather than an idiosyncratic move, and one doomed to failure, we see this as a form of *heresy*. Heresy '(the word itself, containing the idea of a choice, implies this) tends to open up the future' (Bourdieu, 2000: 235). Orthodoxy, by contrast, works 'by closing down the range of possibilities so as to try to induce the belief that "the chips are down forever"' (idem). We believe that socio-analysis is a powerful symbolic transgression. To be effective (rather than rejected as absurd, idiosyncratic or simply ignored or mocked) it has to be 'aimed at challenging the objective structures' and 'to have some chance of being recognized as legitimate (if not reasonable) and to be seen as exemplary, the structures that are contested must themselves be in a state of uncertainty' (Bourdieu, 2000: 236). All academic fields within a regime of neoliberal practices and policies (or at least those fields that suffer the most now, including language education, humanities and sociology), no longer offer for a great number of agents a 'quasi-perfect coincidence between the objective tendencies and subjective expectations [which] make the experience of the world a continuous interlocking of confirmed expectations' (Bourdieu, 2000: 234). A world with a stable future within academic fields and beyond no longer exists and habitus is more likely to be experienced as hysteresis:

> The presence of the past in this kind of false anticipation of the future performed by the habitus is, paradoxically, most clearly seen when the sense of the probable future is belied and when dispositions ill-adjusted to the objective changes because of a hysteresis effect ... are negatively sanctioned because the environment they encounter is too different from the one to which they are objectively adjusted.
> Bourdieu, 1990: 62.

As such, a destabilised habitus, 'torn by contradiction and internal division, generating suffering' (Bourdieu, 2000: 160) and full of 'mismatches, discordances and misfirings' (idem) provides a ripe opportunity for change.

Chapter 3 on neoliberalism, universities and academics and the short summary of prevalent issues in EAP provide sufficient evidence and encouragement to persist with thinking that the structures are uncertain and can be challenged and this challenge is *reasonable*. Reflexivity, as enacted through socio-analysis of the field of EAP, risks destroying the very illusio of the field (Bourdieu, 2000: 12) and risks disillusionment with sentiments of, for example, 'blighted hope' or 'frustrated promise' (Bourdieu, 1984: 150). However, 'to reveal the sacred as profane' (Maton, 2005: 102) promises a more truthful and scientific account of the field of EAP for its practitioners. It also, importantly, illuminates forms of injustices and domination in the field and thereby triggers the possibility of an informed and collective resistance to dominant forces and drive the transformation of the field by its practitioners. However, it would be very naïve to assume that reality can be transformed simply through a change in language or theory, naïve to undertake a purely performative celebration of 'resistance', and naïve to 'ignore the extraordinary inertia which results from the inscription of social structures in bodies' (Bourdieu, 2000: 172).

HERETICAL SCHOLARSHIP AS ETHICS

Turning to what can be done, and this applies to all in language education whether the field structure is similar to or different from that of EAP (in the UK), we posit that *ethics* can provide an *illusio*—making the game worth the candle—with its own investments and rewards. A powerful and generative foundational ethical axiom can be articulated as follows:

> [T]he core values of professional communities revolve around the expectation that we do not keep secrets, whether of discovery or of grounded doubt.
> Shulman, 2001: 50.

Language education, viewed through its professional ethics, can be seen as a vocation, a calling, a moral imperative and service to students and learning (Servage, 2009). One could/should add a maxim that students and colleagues deserve the best knowledge we can find, create and operationalise. If this forms the illusio of teaching then a number of things can follow.

Firstly, we need to develop *scholarship* that is orientated to harnessing the best knowledge we can find, create and operationalise. We envisage scholarship in broader terms than the scholarship of teaching and learning (SoTL), broader than pedagogic research, both of which risk circumscribing scholarship to more directly practical matters of teaching and learning and neglecting the social and political forces that impact teaching and learning. Nor can it be equated with research, more for symbolic and political rather than semantic reasons. As long as research, within neoliberal regimes, functions to produce often meaningless publications, to generate citations to reward the prolific academic striving for significant social, economic and cultural capital, and as long as research is *about* rather than *for* language education, we need to distinguish scholarship from research to signal playing a different game. A game with different values and different objectives. It is important to stress that this does not mean abandoning, rejecting or denigrating research and researchers. It does not mean refusing to publish in journals, nor does it mean disengaging from research communities and avoiding collaboration, inspiration or advice. What it does mean is operating with a *negative* ethics. This means developing a collective and critical scrutiny of all research (and scholarship) which purports to impact language education and to develop the means to answer back. To hold authors and ideas to account and to push back *publicly* when there are claims which are injurious to language education. The reasons for this negative ethics are multiple: the constant search for novelty and innovation endemic in applied linguistics (how many 'turns' do we need?) that leads to fragmented and possibly trivial knowledge of little use to practice; poor understandings of language teaching; pernicious uses of educators and students for research; misreadings and misuses of theories, ideas or data for language education, and the purposes and rewards for researchers who insist on investigating practitioner research and defining what remediation they need and what role in knowledge production they may have. These immediately come to mind as examples and many more could be given.

If language educators are to be vocal and powerful in critiquing research and by doing so effectively help shape more ethically and socially responsive and responsible research and scholarship communities then language educators, individually and especially collectively, need to have a foundational knowledgebase from which to work with and from. This is contested in our field of EAP, as there are no prerequisite credentials or expertise to enter the field nor any clear agreement on what

practitioners need to know. In addition, in situ training and development is ad hoc and subject to the vagaries of centre micro-politics. The
resources, support, time and opportunities for practitioners to develop,
read, critique research and contribute to scholarship is very uneven in
the field. This gives rise to some practitioners (and we include ourselves
here) having greater opportunities, rewards and recognition as well as
a more powerful voice within the field. Others have significantly more
influence in the field through social and economic capital, for example,
as directors of centres and those occupying prominent roles in associations where there is a tendency to orthodoxy and conservation. The field
struggles practitioners engage in to define the field most advantageous to
their current and prospective configuration of capitals ensure conflicting
directions and emphases for a collective knowledgebase and for conflicting
claims for legitimisation, distinction and power within the field. Scholarship, through reflexive socio-analysis, is a powerful means of bringing
these issues to light and to the attention of the field (and often provoking
discomfort and occasionally hostility within the field).

Parenthetically, much of the evidence and justification for the analysis
above has come through scholarship which we individually, jointly and
with others have already published and presented (cf. Ding & Campion,
2016; Ding & Bruce, 2017; Ding, 2019; Ding et al., 2022; Ding &
Bruce, 2022; Ding & Evans, 2022; Ding, 2022; Ding & Monbec,
2024). Our contributions extend into our everyday professional practices
through our work at the University of Leeds through leading, developing,
and supporting scholarship as well as developing an MA in Teaching
English for Academic Purposes. With BALEAP through our advocacy of
reflexive socio-analysis and engagement with leading scholarship across
the field. And through our participation in an informal global network of
practitioners. We mention this not as a boast nor as a claim to a monopoly
of interest and contribution to addressing these issues but simply to point
out that we have invested a great deal in scholarship on these issues
and in our professional practices. And we have done so with very close
collaborators.

Inspired by Ferguson (1997), Ding and Bruce (2017) argued that the
foundational knowledgebase for practitioners of EAP should consist of
three strands:

> Knowledge of disciplinary cultures and values; a form of knowledge which
> is essentially sociological or anthropological.

Knowledge of the epistemological basis of different disciplines; a form of knowledge which is philosophical in nature.
Knowledge of genre and discourse, which is mainly linguistic in nature.
Ferguson, 1997: 85.

Operationalising these three strands in teaching and scholarship enables a powerful 'specialised' knowledge of disciplines to emerge (Ferguson, 1997: 84). A sophisticated gaze that allows practitioners a potent specialism and role within universities where the entanglements of academic communication within disciplinary epistemological and social forces can be made visible to disciplinary colleagues and students. These entanglements can be analysed, critiqued and questioned, and can lead to (ethical) changes in disciplinary communication practices in teaching, in research, and in polices, and practices. This is the specialism and contribution to universities that language educators can and should make. This outward facing gaze needs to be matched with a reflexive inward facing one where the knowledge of the politics, cultures and values of EAP, the knowledge of the epistemologies of EAP and the linguistic and communicative practices of EAP are part of the habitus and training of practitioners. Reflexivity needs to be inscribed in the habitus of the practitioner/researcher to transcend the social and political unconscious that distorts the objectivity of knowledge within our own field. Reflexivity 'aims at increasing the scope and solidity of social scientific knowledge' (Bourdieu & Wacquant, 1992: 36).

If we are to adhere to an illusio of an ethics for language education this is crucial. We cannot begin to address a myriad of ethical and social justice issues within academia without this knowledgebase and without this reflexivity. Neither can we begin to accrue the academic and cultural capitals, as practitioners through our scholarship, to: firstly, challenge and critique research confidentially, competently and in insightful and effective ways; secondly, use and generate knowledge which is *meaningful* for us, for our students and colleagues, and for the field; thirdly, obtain a more legitimate and powerful *academic* position and status within the larger field of the university that allows us to influence changes to teaching, practices and policies, and, lastly, ensure that EAP, as a field operating at the edge of academic, does not tip over the edge into oblivion and, instead, fulfils a latent potential to operate as a powerful actor in transforming language education in universities.

For now, this is a heretical position, one full of potential but still marginal and heterodox in our field of EAP. We see ourselves aligned to Finlayson's position regarding the role of philosophy as:

> a kind of restless and insatiable troublemaking – a disruptiveness that extends to ourselves, our activities and the institutions to which we belong. Since troublemaking is never going to be much appreciated by those on the receiving end of it, it makes sense to think that if philosophy is not hated or feared, then something has gone wrong.
> Finlayson, 2015: 6.

While we doubt our capacity to induce anything as strong as hatred and fear we recognise resistance to our views. We would then urge those with very differing perspectives and views to make them visible—through scholarship rather than through exercising power over others.

Conclusion

We have not produced a blueprint to overthrow neoliberal universities, nor have we produced a manifesto with righteous condemnation and radical action plans. Nor have we sketched a utopic vision of a future university. Our concerns might seem parochial, minor even. We would urge, beyond engaging in our own fields for change, joining the wider university communities that push for significant changes (and bringing to those communities our expertise). If we do want to see the end of neoliberalism and, indeed, capitalism, that entails commitment as citizens with society as such, beyond the ivory ghetto.

Moreover, tired and anxious of waiting 'for everything to come from others, from the holders of power over the game' (Bourdieu, 2000: 237) we have offered what is, we think, a renewed illusio and ethos for language education. One that does entail *disillusion* but does enable us 'to discern the sites where we do indeed enjoy a degree of freedom and those where we do not' (Bourdieu & Wacquant, 1992: 198–9).

We can, collectively, refuse what appears to be our destiny. We can refuse to make a spectacle of ourselves. We can refuse to play a game we can only lose. We can, but only collectively, make what we do more meaningful, more powerful and more ethical.

REFERENCES

Bourdieu, P. (1984). *Distinction: A social critique of the judgement of taste.* Routledge.

Bourdieu, P. (1990). *The logic of practice.* Stanford University Press.

Bourdieu, P. (2000). *Pascalian meditations.* Stanford University Press.

Bourdieu, P., & Wacquant, L. J. (1992). *An invitation to reflexive sociology.* University of Chicago Press.

Bruce, I. (2021). Towards an EAP without borders: Developing knowledge, practitioners, and communities. *International Journal of English for Academic Purposes: Research and Practice, 2021*(Spring), 23–36.

Cheng, A. (2019). Examining the "applied aspirations" in the ESP genre analysis of published journal articles. *Journal of English for Academic Purposes, 38,* 36–47

Collini, S. (2012). *What are universities for?* Penguin UK.

Di Leo, J. R. (2024). *Dark academe: Capitalism, theory, and the death drive in higher education.* Springer Nature.

Ding, A. (2019). EAP practitioner identity. In H. Ken, L. L. C. Wong, K. Hyland, & L. L. C. Wong (Eds.), *Specialised English* (pp. 63–76). Routledge.

Ding, A. (2022). Bourdieu and field analysis: EAP and its practitioners. In Ding, A. & M. Evans (Eds.), *Social theory for English for academic purposes: Foundations and perspectives* (pp. 155–176). Bloomsbury.

Ding, A., & Campion, G. (2016). EAP teacher development. In Hyland, K. & Shaw (Eds.), *The Routledge handbook of English for academic purposes* (pp. 547–559). Routledge.

Ding, A., & Bruce, I. (2017). *The English for academic purposes practitioner. Operating on the edge of academia.* Palgrave.

Ding, A., & Bruce, I. (2022). Association: Power, politics and policy. In Bruce, I. & B. Bond (Eds.), *Contextualizing English for Academic Purposes in Higher Education: Politics, Policies and Practices* (pp. 183–202). Bloomsbury.

Ding, A., & Evans, M. (Eds.). (2022). *Social theory for English for academic purposes: Foundations and perspectives.* Bloomsbury.

Ding, A., & Monbec, L. (2024). A socio-analysis of English for academic purposes. In A. Ding & L. Monbec (Eds.), *Practitioner agency and identity in English for academic purposes* (pp. 11–46). Bloomsbury.

Ding, A., Bond, B., & Bruce, I. (2022). 'Clearly you have nothing better to do with your time than this': A critical historical exploration of contributions to the BALEAP discussion list. *Journal of English for Academic Purposes, 58,* 101109.

Erickson, M., Hanna, P., & Walker, C. (2021). The UK higher education senior management survey: A statactivist response to managerialist governance. *Studies in Higher Education, 46*(11), 2134–2151.

Ferguson, G. (1997). Teacher education and LSP: The role of specialised knowledge. Teacher education for LSP, 80–89.

Finlayson, L. (2015). *The political is political: Conformity and the illusion of dissent in contemporary political philosophy.* Rowman & Littlefield.

Hamp-Lyons, L. (2011). English for academic purposes. In Hinkel, E. (Ed.), *Handbook of research in second language teaching and learning* (pp. 89–105). Routledge.

Hobbis, G., & Hobbis, S. (2013). "Mon Dieu", Bourdieu: The magic of the academy and its ancestor cults. *Anthropologica, 55,* 441–453.

Hyland, K. (2012). The past is the future with the lights on": Reflections on AELFE's 20th birthday. *Ibérica, Revista De La Asociación Europea De Lenguas Para Fines Específicos, 24,* 29–42.

Hyland, K., & Jiang, F. K. (2021). A bibliometric study of EAP research: Who is doing what, where and when? *Journal of English for Academic Purposes, 49,* 100929.

Leibniz, G. W. (1989). *Monadology.* In R. Ariew & D. Garber (Eds.), *Philosophical essays* (pp. 213–225). Hackett Publishing Company (Original work published 1714).

Liu, Y., & Hu, G. (2021). Mapping the field of English for specific purposes (1980–2018): A co-citation analysis. *English for Specific Purposes, 61,* 97–116.

MacDonald, J. (2016). The margins as third space: EAP teacher professionalism in Canadian universities. *TESL Canada Journal, 34*(1), 106–116.

Maton, K. (2005). The sacred and the profane: The arbitrary legacy of Pierre Bourdieu. *European Journal of Cultural Studies, 8*(1), 101–112.

Riazi, A. M., Ghanbar, H., & Fazel, I. (2020). The contexts, theoretical and methodological orientation of EAP research: Evidence from empirical articles published in the Journal of English for academic purposes. *Journal of English for Academic Purposes, 48,* 100925.

Servage, L. (2009). The scholarship of teaching and learning and the neo-liberalization of higher education: Constructing the "Entrepreneurial Learner." *Canadian Journal of Higher Education, 39*(2), 25–43.

Shulman, L. (2001). From Minsk to Pinsk: Why a scholarship of teaching and learning? *Journal of the Scholarship of Teaching and Learning, 1,* 48–53.

Stypinska, D. (2020). *On the genealogy of critique: Or how we have become decadently indignant.* Routledge.

Swales, J. M. (2019). The futures of EAP genre studies: A personal viewpoint. *Journal of English for Academic Purposes, 38,* 75–82.

Watson, D. (2009). *EBOOK: The question of morale: Managing happiness and unhappiness in university life.* McGraw-Hill Education (UK).

Educating for Agency and Solidarity: A Social Semiotics Knowledge Base

Abstract Chapter 6, *Educating for Agency and Solidarity: A social semiotics knowledge base,* describes powerful knowledge to develop positive and critical multiliteracies. The chapter explains what a functional language ontology looks like in curriculum and teaching practice. Leaning on Systemic Functional Linguistics, Systemic Functional Semiotics and Legitimation Code Theory, the chapter details a body of semiotics resources from Genre, Discourse Semantics and Lexicogrammar to multimodality, register variety and a framework to analyse knowledge which a language educator can use both to analyse their students and disciplinary colleagues' needs (in EAP contexts for example) and to design curriculum which develops agency and criticality. Examples are provided from disciplines such as Engineering and Music, along with the analytical steps to approach a complex genre such as the Lecture Recital, engaging the multi-framework toolkit. The chapter concludes that beyond the ethics and scholarship advocated in the previous chapter, this type of expanded knowledge base can help develop practitioners' impact on student learning, but also shape their capital, status and influence in higher education.

Keywords Social semiotics · Knowledge base · Multi-framework knowledge base · Systemic Functional Semiotics · Legitimation Code Theory · Technicality

L. Monbec and A. Ding, *Recovering Language in Higher Education,*
https://doi.org/10.1007/978-3-031-76699-2_6

While it is true that the impetus for social change cannot be located in any one single factor, which is another way of saying that each factor has some part to play, the less visible the role of language in the development of consciousness, and the less clear the relation of this to change in societies, the easier it is to maintain the status quo.
Hasan, 1998, p. 30.
Conscious knowledge of language and the way it functions in social contexts [...] enables us to make choices, to exercise control. As long as we are ignorant of language, it and the ideological systems it embraces control us. Learning about language means learning to choose. All choices are political. We don't write or talk just to pass the time away. [...] Knowledge is power. Meaning is choice. Please choose.
J R Martin (1989, p.62)

Introduction

Having considered elements such as language ontology, legitimation practices and pedagogy, the role of ethics and social analysis as key to understanding the way things are, and provided in the previous chapter an outline of an ethics for the language educator, this chapter provides, not an approach to language education but an outline of a knowledge base we see as key to supporting agency and social change. This chapter then, is about *recovering* knowledge and its centrality to educational endeavours—powerful knowledge, knowledge that deepens thinking, that enables questioning, that liberates. In the previous chapter, it was argued that this knowledge base should include an understanding of social and political educational contexts, and of ethics. This chapter continues from this and details a social semiotic knowledge base which enables the development of critical and positive literacy as well as critical consciousness. This revaluing of knowledge, ethics and solidarity is, perhaps, in our current higher education environment, what Apple called 'heretical thinking' (2009). Another unorthodox element of our proposal is that we will argue that the language teacher or the practitioner is central to this endeavour, perhaps the most likely agent to address the increasing knowledge blindness in practices, and meaninglessness in academic publications (in our field, in any case) imposed by managerial universities and REF measured research (Alvesson et al., 2017). This chapter first outlines broad aspirations for a literacy that develops a solidary consciousness and agency. It then provides a more detailed description of the knowledge base that is useful to recontextualise these aspirations in a workable literacy curriculum. It provides examples of materials and steps for interdisciplinary scholarship and concludes with a discussion of the positions and potential of the teacher in higher education in effecting change.

CRITICAL POSITIVE MULTILITERACIES

In Chapter 4, we analysed different pedagogies aimed at social transformation. Here, we take inspiration from a range of approaches that would be classified as subversive because of their visible pedagogy and explicit knowledge. A key example of such an approach is Hasan's Reflection Literacy, which recontextualises her understanding of semiotics, consciousness and social reproduction to 'create in the pupil an understanding of reading and writing as bearers of deep social significance, not simply as a vehicle for information but as a potent instrument of social formation' (Hasan, 2003, p. 446). This literacy puts at the heart of education a reflection on how language and semiotic resources make meanings that shape our world (including whose interests are served), our consciousness, and equip us to make ethical decisions that serve the planet and its inhabitants. It is a literacy that encompasses multiple semiotic resources, that aims to develop consciousness and higher mental functions, to enable critique, both negative and positive, and to address urgent needs to safeguard against discourse and practices that garner support for destructive ideologies.

Multiliteracies

This view of literacy echoes the work done by the New London Group (1996) and further developments that account for technological innovation (for example Cope & Kalantzis, 2009, 2023; Tavares, 2024) and which stress the need to extend narrow views of literacy to multiteracies, valuing multilingualism, multimodality, multi-repertoires and multi registers (as we argued in Chapter 4). Cope and Kalantzis, in their quest to educate for social justice, see epistemic capital defined as 'capacities for knowledge as social action required for rewarding work, effective social participation, and personal meaning' (2023, p. 4) as the key contributor to social outcome. Developing meaning-making capacities or multiliteracies is for them key to equipping learners with this epistemic capital.

Consciousness and Higher Mental Functions

This view of literacy encompasses Vygotsky's understanding of the role of semiotics in the development of consciousness and higher mental functions, and Bernstein's socio-historical explanation of the relation between a subject and their context and how a subject 'comes to have a sense of what a context is the context for' (Hasan, 2005, p. 36). For Hasan, language should be central to the curriculum, as content carrier but also as process of learning, and as a tool to develop consciousness, echoing concepts such as Critical Language Awareness (Clark et al., 1991). Hasan (2005) explains this through the Vygotskyan concept of semiotic mediation: 'the mediation by someone of something to someone else by means of the modality of language' (2005, p. 195)—Hasan keeps Vygotsky's prioritisation of language over other modalities in this process. For Hasan, semiotic mediation is what language does: it 'enable[s] the speaking subjects to internalise the world they experience in the living of their life' (2005, p. 196), and so inculcates mental dispositions, ways of thinking through a process of interaction with others in the social activities. Hasan differentiates *visible* semiotic mediation (where a learning goal is clearly mediated), and *invisible* semiotic mediation (where what is being mediated is not explicit within the process of everyday, ordinary, activity). Taken together, these manifestations of semiotic mediation both create and maintain culture and enable people to live within it.

Critique Both Negative and Positive

Hasan argues that to understand how political movements and economic decisions such as globalisation, neoliberalism might affect our lives, 'we will need a form of literacy that goes beyond simple interpretation to reflection on the social significance of acts of meanings: literacy must enable one to decide whose meanings are voiced in which acts of semiosis and for whose benefits' (2003, p. 433). As Klein explains in her 2023 book *Doppelganger*, the current global political context has made plain that language is implicated in gathering support for authoritarian ideologies through propaganda, speech control, and misinformation campaigns (Klein, 2023). Klein shows that far-right and populists distort words and mock concepts once held true (for example, *genocide*), to the point that Orwell's Newspeak in *1984* is really no fiction at all. She also shows that liberal democrats are guilty too of this devaluing of words in the sense that they use them without any intention to act upon them. Klein argues that despite years of changing the discourse on an incredibly wide range of issues (gender, Palestine rights, climate breakdown, billionaires and oligarchic rule, neoliberalism...), things have only become worse (p.153). She writes 'the fascists have totally taken our language. I feel speechless' (p. 151), and argues 'words are no longer doing what we expect them to do' (p.151). This is not a very hopeful premise for presenting literacy and knowledge of language as a way towards social transformation. But one thing that Klein does not seem to have access to is a linguistics powerful enough to describe and perhaps address this (an ontological vagueness or default which by now might appear familiar to the reader). We might at least argue that this dissociation between words and reality (p156) is exactly why we need to take care of language education even more, provided that we are equipped with a language ontology that empowers us.

The development of a critical consciousness leans on not simply an awareness of the discursive strategies utilised in hegemonic texts, but also, perhaps more importantly, on what works in discourses of resistance, and solidarity. Here Positive Discourse Analysis work is useful. Martin, who first used the term, discusses the need to supplement Critical Discourse Analysis with Positive Discourse Analysis (Martin, 2004; Bartlett, 2017) or a focus on discursive strategies that express empathy, build solidarity and enable reconciliation. This can be done through '*genre renovation*' (creating new genres which include human experience, and marginalised voices), and a focus on understanding *evaluative language* to express values, feelings, affiliation and *narratives* to highlight issues and inspire change (Martin, 2004). (*Genre renovation*, however, must be implemented with care. As was discussed in Chapter 2, simply changing assignment genres without making clear the basis of achievement is not effective). In Macgilchrist (2007), five strategies are suggested to challenge dominant media frames and discourses: logical inversion, parody, complexification, partial reframing and radical reframing. Hughes (2018), following from Martin, calls for a better understanding of the semiotics of resistance and empowerment through the Action Implicative Discourse Analysis (AIDA) model which aims to analyse problems and the discursive strategies used to address them. Ecolinguistics (Stibbe, 2014) is also linked to PDA and aims to promote the discursive mechanisms that construe the worldviews and behaviours that can preserve the conditions for life on our planet. All these proposals rest on an ontology of language that sees it as a social semiotic resource, part of the social construction of reality. Halliday used the term *ecolinguistics*, after analysing how English construes nature and our relation to it, that it builds in our consciousness natural resources such as water or air as abundant and unlimited through grammatical uncountability, for example, and human power and agency over nature as unquestioned through transitivity systems (Law & Matthiessen, 2019).

We are left with simple tools for resistance: language, knowledge and ethics. To recontextualise these broad aspirations in educational contexts, to inform classroom practice and policy and to equip students with the agency and the strategies to redesign discourse requires a specific knowledge base for language educators and practitioners. This is what we turn to in the next section.

Social Semiotics, Social Theory and Ethics as Knowledge Common

Moving from broad aspirations as outlined above to concrete proposals is where ethics and a focus on student agency are paramount. We first clarify what to look out for in terms of language ontology, and detail a social semiotics knowledge that encompasses genre, discourse semantics, lexicogrammar, multimodality and register variation.

A Functional Language Ontology: What Does This Mean for Teaching?

As we argue in Chapter 2, educators and researchers need to be clear about the language ontology underlying their practices. In our view, a focus on meaning over form, on choice rather than sequence, on context, on registerial decision-making, on power relation and hegemony, on solidarity is the essence of the job of a language educator. An important part of the role then is to teach the ways language/semiotics perpetuates the social world (disciplinary knowledge and epistemology, or power structures for example). Table 6.1 below recaps the main ontological tenets of a linguistic theory like Systemic Functional Linguistics, directly linked to implications for teaching.

Table 6.1 Ontological concepts and teaching implications

Ontological concept	Implication for teaching. Language educators should:
Language is a **resource** we select from to make **meaning** depending on the **context of communication**	Teach meaning-making as the core purpose. This means lessons should explore and answer questions like: • *What meaning is being made?* • *How is meaning made?* (form, including multimodal, is discussed here, and how different form contributes to different meaning) • *Why is this meaning made in this way?* (contextual analysis, audience, interest, power relation, intention...) Teach language as a system of choices made depending on the context and purpose of communication (developing agency). This means we can include when useful the options that were available and the choices that were not made
Meaning-making involves a range of multimodal resources	Expand your teaching repertoire to include all the semiotic resources that are relevant in the genres you teach and how the visual/aural resources interact with verbal resources to make the overall meaning
A social theory of language: Language **construes** our world and **enacts** our social relations (including ideology)	Teach the salient resources that typically construe the disciplinary knowledge (ways the concepts are categorised, defined and related) and its interpersonal relations (ways arguments are developed and engagement with other scholars is conducted) Teach language as a tool for critique, for revealing bias and discrimination in discourse, and for strategic change

(continued)

Table 6.1 (continued)

Ontological concept	Implication for teaching. Language educators should:
Variation: Language choices vary depending on context	This relates with the form vs function discussion: Teach variation (choice, options) *'why is this feature used and not another in this context?'*, not prescriptive rules nor templates: one text analysed with students is only one instance of the linguistic systems realising a specific and precise context of communication. Systems of meanings are abstract, and their linguistic realisations in texts vary according to context. Keep in sight the different selections from the systems that could have been made in different contexts
Language has evolved to meet our needs	Acknowledge that academic discourse is not arbitrary and has evolved to communicate abstract and technical knowledge. This doesn't mean it should not be critiqued, indeed academic discourse has normalised certain ideological constructs, which should be discussed. However, dismissing typical academic genres or features (such as the passive, nominalisations and noun-based grammar) as unecessary is not helpful. Instead, students can benefit from learning register variation
Individuals' repertoire vary and evolve	Make a clear distinction between *registers* (as everyone's tools towards agency) and individual/local *repertoire*, each of which is to be visibly valued in the classroom through a range of approaches including multilingualism and translanguaging. Diversify the registers taught in the classroom: include a range of non-standard registers. Also teach powerful registers, including those giving access to the discourse and practices of powerful institutions. Teach the range of choices available and their social impact

(continued)

Table 6.1 (continued)

Ontological concept	Implication for teaching. Language educators should:
Language is learned through social interaction	Encourage a socio-constructivist (Vygotsky) approach which models texts, guides students through deconstruction, scaffolded joint construction to independent construction and makes semiotics resources visible (see the Teaching and Learning Cycle in SFL/Genre Pedagogy)
Language is social action, and is theorised at multilevel: Genre (social purpose), Discourse Semantics (whole text) Lexicogrammar (clause) and phonology	Teach language from Genre, whole texts, discourse semantics to lexicogrammar (sentence level) Teach language patterns over texts (not just isolated items such as verb forms at clause level) Teach sentence level lexicogrammar as contextualised within a text, its purpose, and audience Try to connect the Lexicogrammar content to Discourse Semantics, Genre and Context to keep both the social and the semiotics in sight (i.e. to reflect the ontological tenet that language reflects construes and enacts social context, that language relates to society) Include discourse semantics (patterns over whole texts/sections of texts). In EAP, for example, an ESP Genre approach might simply provide attention to audience awareness, communicative purpose and 'moves', then to (limited) lexicogrammar forms like verb forms or nominalisations, missing out whole text meanings of identification, appraisal, conjunction, ideation and periodicity (see below)
Language serves 3 main functions (ideational, interpersonal and textual metafunctions)	Teach ideational, interpersonal and textual meaning resources as a way to systematically analyse and understand the role of language in construing the world and enacting relations. *This means answering the question: what and how is the content expressed, what and how are interpersonal meanings made and how is the text held together?* This tripartite view soon becomes a habit for teachers and students

Teaching for social change seems to us to mean to empower students and develop agency. This must include, we believe, teaching explicitly the registers commonly used in hegemonic discourse that enable to access power and resources. In higher education, this naturally includes academic registers. As Lemke (1990) and many others have argued, students should be taught to 'add registers, and genres' so they can make the meanings they chose to make and have a chance at playing, winning, or changing the game. This, however, must be carefully distinguished from teaching 'standardised' language, a variety that is neither culturally not socially neutral. Language standardisation policies Lemke argues run the risk of acculturating students into an 'upper-middle class culture' alien to them and to most of us and to reify the dominance of an artificial and exclusive register. On the contrary, students should be exposed to a diverse range of registers, including powerful registers within their historical development and these should be taught critically, depending on contexts (schooling, EAP, specific communities). As recommended above through PDA, highlighting successful practices in non-hegemonic discourses should be included. In English for Academic Purposes this might take the form of teaching strategies to explain science to a range of audiences, and to counter anti-science discourse (see below for these strategies). The next section goes into more granular description of what this social semiotics knowledge base might include.

Genre, Discourse Semantics and Lexicogrammar

In Chapter 2 on ontology we explained how a linguistic theory like SFL provides a link from ideology, the social world and language through a connected architecture of description at Genre, Discourse Semantics and Lexicogrammar levels. Table 6.2 lists the typical systems and resources organised by metafunction and by strata, creating what has been called a 3 × 3 grid (Dreyfus et al., 2016) which maps the resources which can be described and taught when salient in a given genre (they do not all come up as salient, hence the need for teachers to have some practice in analysing texts so they can pick the most important features). Table 6.2 is adapted from Dreyfus et al. (2016), but a reader might find different versions in a range of SFL educational linguistics or pedagogical sources (Humphrey, 2016; Monbec, 2020).

A reader might imagine that each of the entries in Table 6.2 above can be explored by accessing discourse research in the genres of schooling for example. And in the SFL tradition, much work has been done to describe whole disciplinary discourse (see Coffin, 2006 for History for example), to describe more delicate items such as the combination of ideational and interpersonal resources in Biology lab reports (Hao & Humphrey, 2009). The 3 × 3 matrix is also only one of the ways to recontextualise SFL architecture for teaching purposes. Other options include Humphrey's (2016), where ideational meanings are divided into experiential and logical functions (which is very useful to focus on logical relations); Monbec (2020) does the same but collapses the columns Discourse Semantics and Lexicogrammar into one to create a table of instantiation/academic writing toolkits which can be used by students in classroom activities.

At this juncture, we refer the reader to a wealth of SFL disciplinary discourse literature and decades of research in SFL/Genre application which look at precise entries in Table 6.2 in terms of analysis, and at a range of pedagogical application and classroom teaching application. For EAP teaching, chances are practitioners can find in the literature analyses of the genres they wish to teach in a range of disciplines (a good place to start for an overview of typical genres across disciplines is Nesi and Gardner, 2012). Monbec (2022) provides a list of sequenced foundational readings to explore SFL recontextualisation in language classrooms. Examples of classroom recontextualisation include instantiation-based approaches (Gardner, 2016; Monbec, 2020) and SFL/Genre-based pedagogy (for example Coffin & Donohue, 2014; Emilia & Hamied, 2015; Dreyfus et al. 2016; Kartika-Ningsih & Gunawan, 2019; Guerra-Lyons & Mendinueta, 2020). Yet, communication needs, and technological innovations mean that the discourse of disciplines is evolving fast, becoming more complex, addressing different audiences, integrating a range of multimedia and multimodal resources. The next section describes elements of an expanded teaching knowledge base which can accommodate these semiotic changes.

EXPANDING THE KNOWLEDGE BASE: MULTIMODALITY, REGISTER VARIETY AND KNOWLEDGE

A first almost banal statement is that students at university are involved in increasingly multimodal communication (in teaching and learning activities and assignment types, for example). From a lab report and its graphs and tables in the results of a Biological Sciences report, to the presentation of a 3D prototype in Design, students are asked to engage with

Table 6.2   3 × 3 grid: semiotic resources

Adapted from Dreyfus et al. (2016) SLATE (3 × 3)	Genre and register (whole text)	Discourse Semantics (phases)	Grammar and expression (clause and sentence level)
Ideational meanings	What are the fields, are they technical, specialised? Do ideas unfold in expected stages: *Context ^1 Analysis/ Evaluation^ Judgement I^M^R^D*	**Ideation**: kinds of activities, participants, classifications **Conjunction**: how activities are connected logically (time, cause, consequence…)	Transitivity Participants and processes (verbal groups) Classification Circumstance Noun group Logicosemantic relations (elaborating, extending, enhancing, projecting)
Interpersonal meanings	Is the text authoritative, impersonal? What are the evaluative meanings made, what/who is evaluated? How are other sources/different voices managed?	**Appraisal**: evaluation, attitudes, strengths of feelings, alignment of readers; Engagement with other sources: distancing, endorsing; Graduation (degree)	Engagement: projection (quoting and reporting), modality, polarity and concession Attitudes: feelings and values, opinions, judgements, overt/ covert
Textual meanings	How is the Information organised and signposted? Is the content previewed and reviewed (intro and conclusion)? How are entities referred to throughout the create cohesion?	**Periodicity**: rhythm of discourse, signposts and consolidation **Identification** (tracking people, places and things)	Theme and New Macro and hyperThemes Lexical chains Deictic and general nouns Tenses

[1] Is an SFL convention which means *is followed by*.

and develop confidence with multimodal semiotic resources. EAP practitioners working in the STEM disciplines, for example, will be familiar with the need for students to draw on visual and verbal resources to clearly articulate the valued knowledge in their disciplines to both specialist and non-specialist audiences. Students commonly use a range of multimodal artefacts such as posters, renderings, drawings, models, exhibits, visualisations, infographics to engage, inform and persuade different audiences and communicate their research, ideas or designs effectively. To teach meaning-making in these disciplines requires teaching multimodal (the orchestration of different semiotic resources) and intersemiotic (the relation between semiotic resources) communication (Monbec & Tilakaratna, 2023; Kress and van Leeuwen, 2020; Bateman, 2008).

Beyond becoming familiar with the types of visuals, graphs and images typical in their disciplines, students need to understand the relation between various semiotic resources, including verbal and non verbal. Theorisation of these relations has used SFL logical semantic relations, such as expansion and elaboration to describe the way a visual relates to the verbal text accompanying it (Royce, 2007). Another perspective on this relation is that of density, specifically how each mode contributes to the packing or unpacking of technical meanings. In Fig. 6.1, drawn from one of the authors' classroom materials, students are asked to think of the relation between the verbal content of an Engineer's TED talk (Sharma, 2020), with the visuals used (including the type, the function, the sequencing and the rhythm) to familiarise them with the decisions they should take as they design their communication artefacts.

A helpful and accessible way to describe the technicality over a presentation or a text, is to use *Semantic Gravity*, a concept from the Legitimation Code Theory, which provides a toolkit to analyse knowledge claims (Maton, 2013). Semantic Gravity has been used in a range of educational contexts to analyse abstraction and technicality as well as concreteness and contextualisation in disciplinary discourse. In a text aimed at a non-specialist audience, Semantic Gravity, represented as a wave in Fig. 6.2 enables students to visualise the content in a talk (or any other text) that is more dense and technical (at the top of the graph), and the content that is less technical and related in some way to the audience's context (at the bottom of the graph). Figure 6.2 is drawn from the author's teaching materials and shows students' group work, each wave representing a group analysis. Students were also asked to paste parts of the script and the visuals to analyse their respective roles in packing or

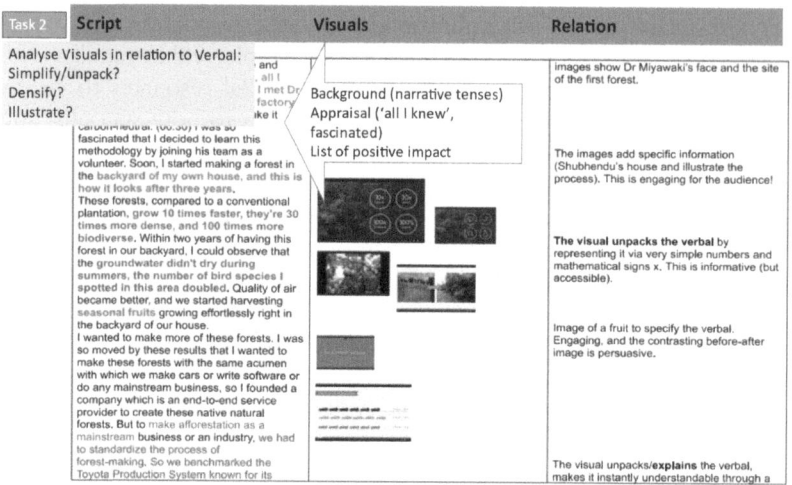

Fig. 6.1 Sample classroom materials on intersemiosis designed based on an Engineering talk

unpacking technicality at each stage of the talk. These are tools which can easily be integrated into a teacher's knowledge base and deployed in needs analysis and pedagogy, and which have proven versatile and impactful in a range of educational settings.

As is shown in the examples of a talk addressed to a non-specialist audience above, academic discourse is seen as encompassing more than the formal and highly dense register aimed at disciplinary experts but also that which addresses more general audiences. There is a great need for academics, and students to communicate their work to a wider audience, and this therefore should be part of language and literacy programmes at university. This calls for an awareness of the semiotic strategies that are commonly used to address different audiences to pack/unpack technicality. The resources involved in making these meanings, on an academic register cline are detailed in Table 6.3 and include the typical register for an expert audience, and those for a non-specialist audience, put in parallel so practitioners and students can see these resources as an adjustment in the choices they make when planning their writing and presentations. It is

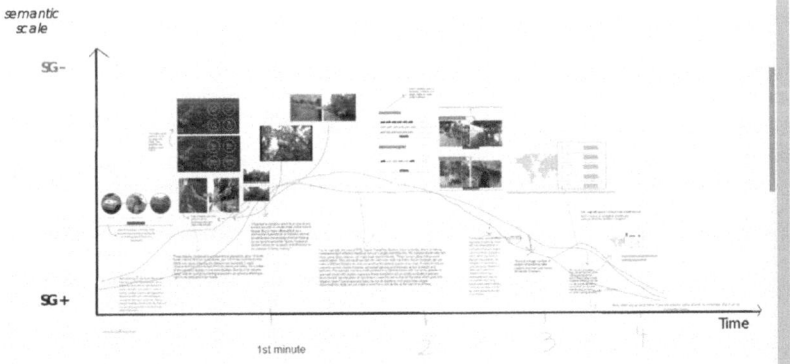

Fig. 6.2 Sample classroom materials on technicality using a Semantic Gravity wave to visualise abstract and concrete meanings in an Engineering talk

very useful to make these visible to students so they see the choices they themselves can make to communicate effectively to different audiences. The table lists the differences at genre and purpose level, and at stages levels, then what lexicogrammar and multimodal resources are used for each of these contexts. Note for example that crafting a message for a non-specialist audience involves much more than omitting technical terms, but affects the grammar of the clause as well, reintroducing human agents and processes as well as conjunction, rather than these being hidden in nominal groups and processes in typical academic discourse. The aim of making these strategies visible is to enable students to move up and down this cline depending on context of communication when writing assignments and preparing presentations for a range of audiences, but also, more spontaneously to address any sign of confusion from an interlocuter or audience.

The Complexification of Higher Education Genres: The Lecture Recital

Above, we listed the linguistic resources which are typically used in academic discourse. A practitioner might find published social semiotics literature that details these resources in specific disciplinary genres to help their analyses. Yet, genres used in higher education have become increasingly varied, diverse, multimodal and specialised. EAP practitioners are also often assigned to different modules and different contexts. Practitioners therefore need to be able to analyse the needs of their

Table 6.3 Academic register cline

Academic Register cline	
Non-specialised audience	Expert audience
Genre: *Engaging, persuading, informing* **Structure**: Problem ^ Solution; Narratives (orientation^ complication^ Resolution)	**Genre**: *Informing, explaining, reporting, arguing* **Expected generic/template structure**: *Research article*: Introduction^Methods^Results^Discussion *Reflection:* Background ^Critical Incident^Excavation^Transformation **Types of Reports**: composition, classifications, sequence, procedures (different generic structures)
Technicality unpacked **Unpacking strategies to explain and make technicality accessible:** • Common sense synonyms (*tiny*-nano) • Similes (*like*) and metaphors (including visual metaphors) • **Congruent (unpacked) grammar**: Include human participants and their actions and thoughts (processes) (congruent grammar vs noun grammar) *'If you play with chemicals, you will...'* • Visuals help unpack (illustrate) Useful expressions: *That means, in other words, this is the same as when...*	*Dense, packed Technicality high* **Expressing technicality (Packed):** • vocabulary is technical (and the reader is expected to understand) • **Noun-based grammar and grammatical metaphor**: Complex noun groups and nominalisations *(*Noun + modifiers and Prepositional phrases*)* +**Logical link** expressed by processes to discuss abstract concepts: *'Increased exposure to chemicals **leads to**...'* • Visuals are technical (often denser than text)
Engaging the audience: Address the audience: Pronouns: *You, your*; questions; imperative: *let's imagine...*	Less engagement with audience/reader but **engagement with the literature** through reporting verbs, citations, distancing/endorsing and evaluative language

students, and the needs of their disciplinary colleagues in quite challenging contexts. This is not new; ESP teaching has always included needs analysis. Yet thorough genre analysis has traditionally been conducted by applied linguists, engaging larger resources in terms of research scope, size of data set and time. The argument here is that practitioners must be equipped with a comprehensive knowledge base to enable them to analyse their students' needs (the genres they have to produce) thoroughly, yet in a flexible and time-sensitive manner, to be able to draw out the key salient meaning-making practices, whether at generic, discourse semantic or lexicogrammar level, whether to express ideation, interpersonal or textual meaning, whether to reach an expert or non-specialist audience, and using a range of multimodal and multimedia resources.

Recently, a colleague from the Language Centre, who teaches academic literacies to master's students in the School of Music at the University of Leeds, brought the *Lecture Recital* genre to our attention. A very well-established genre in music education, it requires students to skilfully synthesise performance and scholarly analysis in an oral presentation. The genre is extremely complex and demands much mastery in argumentation, performance, orchestration of multimodal evidence and presentation skills. It is both fascinating and daunting. It must be exhausting too, as these recitals can last close to a whole hour! Where does one begin to help students prepare for this type of high stake communication?

Watching several samples, both student and professional, gives a general understanding of the genre: the purpose is to demonstrate knowledge, sensibility, analytical and critical skills, and communicative competence, around a thesis chosen by the student. The micro or embedded genres within this broad macro genre might include a *historical account* to situate the influences on a given composer, and *argument* (students often say *I argue that*), and a range of evidence to support this argumentation which include verbal and visuals such as music scores, themselves often annotated for salient elements, images, slides and, of course, extended performance.

A practitioner might be able to increase their the genre through a more thorough genre analysis. At best this will be incorporated in an interdisciplinary scholarship project, which, with appropriate ethics clearance, will give access to a large set of student samples at 2 or 3 levels of achievement so comparison can be drawn, and to disciplinary expertise through focus groups with disciplinary colleagues. For an example of this type of interdisciplinary collaboration around the genre of Critical Reflection in Nursing, see Tilakaratna et al. (2020), Brooke (2019), Monbec et al. (2021) and Tilakaratna (2024). This is an example of where the meaningful scholarship encouraged in the previous chapter can materialise. At worse, practitioners might be able to access samples and conduct the analysis in isolation. Still, this will benefit students and the resulting pedagogical materials might convince the disciplinary colleague that collaboration is worth the effort.

Toolkit for Interdisciplinary Scholarship

In the best-case scenario mentioned above, that of collaboration with disciplinary lecturers, and literacy/EAP lecturers, the following scholarship project can be conducted:

Step 1: Discuss with the disciplinary lecturer the purpose of the assignment,[2] the audience, what they want to see, what they want students to avoid (in other words, try to understand the lecturer's perspective on the basis of achievement, what they value in these assignments). The toolkit above should enable practitioners to steer the conversation to meaning and meaning-making resources (away from language accuracy or surface issues), and to the purpose and ways the discipline's knowledge and values are best communicated.

Step 2: The genre should be analysed for its function within the broader culture and critiqued. For example, does this genre favour specific students, and what can be done to address this beyond making the basis of achievement visible? What does the genre reveal about the discipline's epistemology and its values?

Step 3: Collect samples following appropriate ethical procedures. Classify the samples into levels of achievement and anonymise all scripts. Begin the analysis with the best samples (according to the lecturers). An SFL/Genre analysis will begin with the context, the purpose, the audience, what is valued, how is the audience engaged, informed and persuaded? It will move to the stages that are used to achieve this purpose and will then move to Discourse Semantics systems and their lexicogrammar realisation. Ideational, interpersonal and textual resources will be analysed to understand what type of disciplinary knowledge is valued, what type of evaluation is expected, how the student is to assert a certain authority and how cohesion is built through the various stages and modes. Because of limited resources, practitioners can first focus on a few samples, and then focus on the semiotic resources which appear to be salient.

Step 4: Multimodal resources can be analysed around the types that are used and their function, how they are designed and annotated and how they are integrated into the verbal element of the text or presentation.

---

[2] This could be any pedagogical issue encountered in the discipline, such as showing critical thinking in assignment, or reflective skills (however the subject lecturer phrases this, the multi-toolkit analysis presented can help reveal what is valued in the genre or the practice, and what students seem to be struggling with (and subject lecturers struggling to explain in literacy terms).

Step 5: Intersemiosis analysis means relating the verbal and visual or aural resources, and analysing what each mode contributes, and how modes collaborate towards the overall meaning.

Step 6: Ways technicality is managed should be analysed too, and this could be part of the SFL/Genre analysis above as part of the ideational resources analysis, but if it is key in the genre, then dealing with it on its own, with a concept such as Semantic Gravity might have clear pedagogical benefits. What semiotic resources are used to pack/unpack the technicality?

Step 7: Once salient resources that seem typical of the genre and necessary to achieve the purpose of communication are located in high performing samples, the analyst should compare the findings with mid and low performance samples. Compare findings with the other analysts on the Literacy/EAP team.

Step 8: The findings can be compiled and should be discussed with the disciplinary expert to get better insights into the patterns observed. By then the discussion will be around what it is high achieving students are able to do with semiotic resources to express the knowledge and values of the discipline, which lower achieving students are struggling with.

Step 9: Devise output from the project in the form of pedagogical resources for students and for disciplinary colleagues. Use examples drawn from the samples and the analysis.

Step 10: Publish findings to help other practitioners who might be teaching the same genre.

The above 1–9 steps represent a way to recontextualise theory in practice. In this case the theories and frameworks recontextualised are multiple to account for the complexity of the genre. Being equipped with this type of knowledge and the ability to perform these types of analyses so they can inform teaching and learning, and collaboration with colleagues across the disciplines, can be transformative for the field, the practitioners' position and their status in higher education. This is what we turn to in the last section of the chapter.

CONCLUSION: LANGUAGE TEACHERS
AND PRACTITIONERS' CAPITAL

Martin (1997, p. 411) talks about the 'teacher linguist' and describes how teachers doing their MA in Sydney University were trained in Halliday's social semiotics, along other modules on general linguistics, sociolinguistics, language development and curriculum, pedagogy, and testing. He explains how these students went on to do PhDs that altogether set up a new 'educational linguistics transdiscipline'. In EAP, this is the type of work and the type of identity for EAP practitioners which might be highly beneficial (for students and all involved). In this chapter, we have tried to present a way to do this in English for Academic Purposes, or Academic Literacy in Higher Education, which emphasises an interaction with the discipline based on deep knowledge of social semiotics and disciplinary practices, values and epistemology.

One way to develop this specialism in practitioners, as mentioned in Chapter 5, consists of equipping practitioners with a mixed framework analytical toolkit which we have started sketching here. This is feasible if resources are made available for practitioners to develop themselves. This involves a repositioning of the practitioner, perhaps daunting for some, depending on their knowledge, their orientation to a specific language ontology as explained in Chapter 2, to operate a shift from a focus on form and accuracy, to a focus on meaning-making and communicating the disciplinary knowledge and values. When we think in terms of meaning-making and develop theoretical and analytical expertise, we become central to the university and have some epistemic capital to level. This epistemic capital also expands through scholarship: engaging in scholarship, building the expertise to do scholarship, and collaborating to make different expertise converge.

Part of this repositioning of practitioners also involves pushing back where possible. In *Academic Irregularities*, Morrish and Staunston (2019) call for language to be used carefully (this argument for those who see language as construing and enacting is unsurprising). They recommend avoiding the repetition of empty managerial talk and changing the metaphors (as well as undoing the naturalisation of current metaphors). Hasan states that 'casual conversation abounds in […] explicit aphorisms' (2005, p. 201). Aphorisms deserve conscious deliberate reflection and unpacking. This is where analysing others' success in doing the same can be useful (see Positive Discourse Analysis). It's perhaps not surprising that PDA's better-known texts are those that point to discrimination but emphasise solidarity and reconciliation: developing an ethics which combats competitiveness and divisiveness and values collaboration will be crucial to the success of the endeavour.

Critique also needs to be robust against unfair and dismissive representations of practitioners, for example as 'good enough' (but less good than) researchers. Hasan (2005, p.202) argues that some actions and discourse are ancillary, while others are constitutive of a culture, and of mental habits. Practitioners need to contest what is constitutive using the best evidence, knowledge and argumentation available. Then, the advantage of practitioners' positions in the field, impacting students' experiences and learning, and engaging with theory and scholarship, will become more evident or easier for practitioners to at least imagine.

References

Alvesson, M., Gabriel, Y., & Paulsen, R. (2017). *Return to meaning: A social science with something to say.* Oxford University Press.

Apple, M. W. (2009). Can critical education interrupt the right? *Discourse: Studies in the Cultural Politics of Education, 30*(3), 239–251. https://doi.org/10.1080/01596300903036814

Bartlett, T. (2017). Positive discourse analysis. In J. Flowerdew & J. Richardson (Eds.), *The Routledge handbook of critical discourse studies* (pp. 133–147). Routledge.

Bateman, J. A. (2008). *Multimodal documents and genre.* Palgrave.

Brooke, M. (2019). Using Semantic Gravity profiling to develop critical reflection. *Reflective Practice, 20*(6), 808–821.

Clark, R., Fairclough, N., Ivanič, R., & Martin-Jones, M. (1991). Critical language awareness part II: Towards critical alternatives. *Language and Education, 5*(1), 41–54. https://doi.org/10.1080/09500789109541298

Coffin, C. (2006). *Historical discourse.* Continuum.

Coffin, C., & Donohue, J. (2014). *A language as social semiotic-based approach to teaching and learning in higher education.* Wiley-Blackwell.

Cope, B., & Kalantzis, M. (2009). "Multiliteracies": New literacies, new learning. *Pedagogies: an International Journal, 4*(3), 164–195. https://doi.org/10.1080/15544800903076044

Cope, B., & Kalantzis, M. (2023). Towards education justice: The multiliteracies project revisited. In G. Zapata, M. Kalantzis & B. Cope (Eds.), *Multiliteracies in international educational contexts* (pp. 1–33). Routledge.

Dreyfus, S. J., Humphrey, S., Mahboob, A., & Martin, J. R. (2016). *Genre Pedagogy in Higher Education: The SLATE Project*. Basingstoke: Palgrave Macmillan.

Emilia, E., & Hamied, F. A. (2015). Systemic functional linguistic genre pedagogy (SFL GP) in a tertiary EFL writing context in Indonesia. *TEFLIN Journal, 26*(2), 155.

Gardner, S. (2016). A genre-instantiation approach to teaching English for specific academic purposes: Student writing in business, economics and engineering. *Writing and Pedagogy, 8*(1), 117–144.

Guerra-Lyons, J. D., & Mendinueta, N. R. (2020). On the notion of "owning a forest": Ideological awareness and genre-based pedagogy in university critical literacy. *DELTA: Documentação De Estudos Em Lingüística Teórica e Aplicada, 36*(4), 2020360412–2020360421.

Hasan, R. (1998). The disempowerment game: Bourdieu and language in literacy. *Linguistics and Education, 10*(1), 25–87.

Hasan, R. (2003). Globalization, literacy and ideology. *World Englishes, 22*(4), 433–448.

Hasan, R. (2005). *Language society and consciousness* (Vol. 1). J. Webster (Ed.). Equinox.

Hao, J., & Humphrey, S. (2009). The role of 'coupling' in biological experimental reports. *Linguistics and the Human Sciences, 5*(2), 169–195.

Hughes, J. M. F. (2018). Progressing positive discourse analysis and/in critical discourse studies: Reconstructing resistance through progressive discourse analysis. *Review of Communication, 18*(3), 193–211.

Humphrey, S. (2016). *Academic literacies in the middle years: A framework for enhancing teacher knowledge and student achievement*. Routledge.

Kartika-Ningsih, H., & Gunawan, W. (2019). Recontextualisation of genre-based pedagogy: The case of Indonesian EFL classrooms. *Indonesian Journal of Applied Linguistics, 9*(2), 335–347.

Klein, N. (2023). *Doppelganger: A trip into the mirror world*. Knopf Canada.

Kress, G., & Van Leeuwen, T. (2020). *Reading images: The grammar of visual design*. Routledge.

Law, L. H. L., & Matthiessen, C. M. (2019). Revisiting Halliday's (1990) 'New ways of meaning: The challenge to applied linguistics': What has changed and what still needs to be done? In *The Conference on Language and Ecology: Towards a Shared Narrative in Interdisciplinary Research*. Hong Kong Shue Yan University.

Lemke, J. L. (1990). Literacy and diversity. In R. Giblett & J. O'Carroll (Eds.), *Discipline, dialogue, difference* (pp. 147–169). Duration Publications.

Macgilchrist, F. (2007). Positive discourse analysis–contesting dominant discourse by reframing the issues. *Critical Approaches to Discourse Analysis across Disciplines, 1*(1), 74–94.

Martin, J. R. (1989). *Factual Writing: exploring and challenging social reality.* Oxford University Press.

Martin, J. R. (1997). Linguistics and the consumer: The practice of theory. *Linguistics and Education, 9*(4), 411–448.

Martin, J. R. (2004). Positive discourse analysis: Solidarity and change. *Revista Canaria De Estudios Ingleses, 49,* 179–200.

Maton, K. (2013). *Knowledge and knowers: Towards a realist sociology of education.* Routledge.

Monbec, L. (2020). Systemic functional linguistics for the EGAP module: Revisiting the common core. *Journal of English for Academic Purposes, 43,* 100794.

Monbec, L. (2022). Systemic functional linguistics for the self-taught. *BALEAP research and publication blog.* https://research.baleap.org/2022/06/29/systemic-functional-linguistics-for-the-self taught part 2/?_thumbnail_id=393

Monbec, L., & Tilakaratna, N. (2023). Multimodal communication in a design and engineering EMI module. Presented at the BALEAP PIM on Multimodality in EAP, St Andrews University.

Monbec, L., Tilakaratna, N., Brooke, M., Lau, S. T., Chan, Y. S., & Wu, V. (2021). Designing a rubric for reflection in nursing: A legitimation code theory and systemic functional linguistics-informed framework. *Assessment & Evaluation in Higher Education, 46*(8), 1157–1172. https://doi.org/10.1080/02602938.2020.1855414

Morrish, L., & Sauntson, H. (2019). *Academic irregularities: Language and neoliberalism in higher education.* Routledge.

Nesi, H., & Gardner, S. (2012). Genres across the disciplines: Student writing in higher education. Cambridge: Cambridge University Press.

New London Group. (1996). A pedagogy of multiliteracies: Designing social futures. *Harvard Educational Review, 66,* 60–92. https://doi.org/10.17763/haer.66.1.17370n67v22j160u

Royce, T. D. (2007). Intersemiotic complementarity: A framework for multimodal discourse analysis. In T. Royce & W. Bowcher (Eds.), *New directions in the analysis of multimodal discourse* (pp. 63–109). Routledge.

Sharma, S. (2020). An engineer's vision for tiny forests, everywhere [Video]. *TED conferences.* https://www.ted.com/talks/shubhendu_sharma_an_engineer_s_vision_for_tiny_forests_everywhere

Stibbe, A. (2014). An ecolinguistic approach to critical discourse studies. *Critical Discourse Studies, 11*(1), 117–128.

Tavares, V. (Ed.). (2024). *Social justice through pedagogies of multiliteracies: Developing and strengthening L2 learner agency and identity.* Taylor & Francis.

Tilakaratna, N. (2024). Developing disciplinary values: Interdisciplinary approaches to investigating critical reflection writing in undergraduate nursing. In N. Tilakaratna & E. Szenes (Eds.), *Demystifying critical reflection* (pp. 21–40). Routledge.

Tilakaratna, N. L., Brooke, M., Monbec, L., Lau, S. T., Wu, V. X., & Chan, Y. S. (2020). Insights into an interdisciplinary project on critical reflection in nursing: Using SFL and LCT to enhance SoTL research and practice. In R. C. Plews & M. L. Amos (Eds.), *Evidence-based faculty development through the scholarship of teaching and learning (SoTL)* (pp. 303–327). IGI Global.

CHAPTER 7

Conclusion

Abstract This chapter, as a conclusion to the volume, evokes the interconnectedness of agents, and the relation of our educational practices with our social world .ics The chapter also discusses the compatibility of the theories underpinning the discussions in the volume: Social Semiotics and Field Theory, as well as ethics. We explain that beyond a common reference to the term illusion, it is through agency that these theories connect. Both Social Semiotics/SFL and Bourdieu's Field Theory (despite frequent interpretations of Bourdieu as determinist) consider the potential for individual agency and the possibility for change, through the ethical choices open to us in daily encounters, and this despite the weight of our habitus and of our semiotic practices or coding orientations. For both Bourdieu and social semioticians, the hope lies in our capacity to bring things to consciousness. Perhaps the main illusion we wanted to dispel in this volume is that of powerlessness. Our sphere of influence might be small: our peers, our leadership, our colleagues, our students but in any of our daily interactions in our own classrooms and with colleagues lies a possibility.

Keywords Social semiotics · SFL · Field theory · Agency · Choice · Illusion · Change

L. Monbec and A. Ding, *Recovering Language in Higher Education*, https://doi.org/10.1007/978-3-031-76699-2_7

The illusion of the powerlessness of language in construing reality, quite paradoxically, becomes the greatest source of its power: it becomes the most powerful instrument for the maintenance of ideology.
Ruqaiya Hasan (1988) (as cited in Lukin, 2019)

Throughout the volume we have tried to provide ways to break through binaries and to question doxa, with the aim to operate a metanoia, breaking from the illusio. From language ontology, to ethics, and pedagogy, we hope that we've managed to show a world where our practices are interconnected with the broader sociocultural structure. Educational practices are shaped by knowledge that has been made available to us, which in turn is shaped by legitimation forces in the broader socio and political realm. Our decisions are then shaped by our own habitus, and a range of ethical entanglements (Bond, 2024),

To explore this, we have brought two theories, two ways of thinking about the world—Bourdieu's Field Theory and Social Semiotics in a dialogue. In providing a way to theorise the relation between language and society, these theories have enabled us to consider issues of language in higher education in a productive dialectic that has involved semiotics, social structure, ethics and consciousness. This combination of theories allowed us to keep in sight the broader social, political and ethical concerns that bear upon educational practices and to detail a social semiotics knowledge base and ethics which might provide a way forward.

A central concept in the volume is illusio, a term which comes up in both Bourdieu's and in social semioticians' work as shown in Hasan's quote above. Unearthing patterns of thoughts, or doxic ways to see the field has aimed to find some degree of clear-sightedness. We also found an alignment between field theory and social semiotics around agency. Both theories consider the potential for individual agency and the possibility for change, through the choices open to us in daily encounters, and this despite the weight of our habitus and of our semiotic practices or coding orientations. For both Bourdieu and social semioticians, the hope lies in our capacity to bring things to consciousness. Perhaps the main illusion we wanted to dispel in this volume is that of powerlessness. Our sphere of influence might be small: our peers, our leadership, our colleagues, our students but in any of our daily interactions in our own classrooms and with colleagues lies a possibility. This book has been, for us, an attempt to speak out, and to communicate optimism and hope (Collini, 2017).

We have discussed and proposed a few concrete ways forward, involving the development (and protection) of a knowledge base for language educators, a social understanding of the field, and a more deliberate consideration of ethics and collective solidarity. With the neoliberal rule of universities and the consequences it has had on curriculum, we are at risk of seeing knowledge disappear, or silenced, especially in the humanities, social sciences, and language disciplines. For those of us critically inclined, we can recognise in this a deliberate intention to erase swathes of knowledge—like authoritarian regimes' control of curriculum and public memory. Knowledge of meaning-making, and of the relation between language and society, we have argued is a common good which should be part of every educational endeavour. Ethics should also be a core concern in the daily choices we are presented with in our professional practices, our scholarship, and our interactions with students and colleagues. When exercising power over curriculum, or systems and policies, ethics should also be at the forefront of decision-making. With a clearer awareness of the social structures influencing our field, and a better understanding of how these impact individual actions and behaviours, it may be possible to develop self-awareness, increased reflexivity and to build a collective and solidary culture in higher education.

REFERENCES

Bond, B. (2024). An exploration of the ethics of scholarship in EAP collegial connections and ethical entanglements. In A. Ding & L. Monbec (Eds.), *Practitioner agency and identity in English for academic purposes.* Bloomsbury.

Collini, S. (2017). *Speaking of universities.* Verso.

Hasan, R. (1988). Language in the process of socialisation: Home and school. In J. Oldenburg, T. van Leeuwen, & L. Gerot (Eds.), *Language and socialisation: Home and school (Proceedings from the working conference on language in education, 17–21 November, 1986)* (pp. 36–96). Macquarie University.

Lukin, A. (2019). *War and its Ideologies.* Springer.

INDEX

A

academic discourse, 30, 39, 40, 122, 128, 129

academic doxa, 51

academic register, 84, 86, 90, 124

academic register cline, 128, 130

academic writing, 18, 39, 76, 125

access, 8, 32, 33, 39, 40, 68, 76, 77, 80, 84, 86, 87, 89–93, 119, 122, 124, 131

accommodation-based theoy(ies), 85

accountability, 53, 56

accuracy, 5, 23, 24, 32, 35, 106, 132, 134

Action Implicative Discourse Analysis (AIDA), 119

affect, 34, 38, 118, 129

agency, 7, 9, 10, 16, 17, 20, 32, 33, 56, 64, 76, 82, 84, 89, 91–94, 104, 116, 117, 120–122, 124, 140

ambitions, 52, 63

aporia, 52

applicability, 93

appropriacy, 5, 35

assessment, 7, 18, 31, 34, 35

assessment criteria, 40

audience awareness, 123

auto-analysis, 107

autonomy, 33, 58, 59, 82

B

Behaviourist pedagogies, 79

Bernstein, Basil, 3, 8, 77, 87

bibliometrics, 61

blogs, 40

Bourdieu, Pierre, 3–5, 8, 10, 26, 47, 49, 50, 53, 58–62, 67, 76, 85, 87, 88, 94, 103, 104, 106–108, 111, 112, 140

Bourdieu's field theory, 4, 6, 140

bullying, 63, 66, 68

C

careerism, 57, 68

Chomsky, N., 20, 24–27, 33, 38

citations, 61, 63, 64, 109, 130

The manufacturer's authorised representative in the EU is Springer
Nature Customer Service Centre GmbH, Europaplatz 3, 69115 Heidelberg,
Germany. If you have any concerns regarding our products, please
contact ProductSafety@springernature.com

Printed and bound by CPI Group (UK) Ltd, Croydon, CR0 4YY

29/04/2026

02099450-0013

The manufacturer's authorised representative in the EU is Springer
Nature Customer Service Centre GmbH, Europaplatz 3, 69115 Heidelberg,
Germany. If you have any concerns regarding our products, please
contact ProductSafety@springernature.com

Printed and bound by CPI Group (UK) Ltd, Croydon, CR0 4YY
29/04/2026
02099450-0013